Ease into It with Edgar Degas

Learn to Draw Book

activibooks for kids
Coloring, Drawing & Activity Books For Children

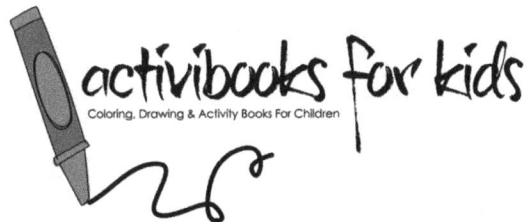

INSTRUCTIONS FOR DRAWING:

THIS HOW-TO DRAWING BOOK CONSISTS OF IMAGES THAT ARE PLACED ON GRIDS. THERE IS A DRAWING BOX LOCATED AT THE LOWER PART OF THE PAGE AND THAT WILL SERVE AS YOUR PRACTICE SPACE. TO COPY THE IMAGE, DRAW PARTS OF THE IMAGE PER GRID AND PUT THEM ON THE BIGGER GRIDS. SOUNDS DIFFICULT? NOT REALLY. TRY IT FIRST!

IT'S OKAY IF YOU DON'T COPY THE IMAGE PERFECTLY. AFTER ALL, DRAWING IS ABOUT THE EXPRESSION OF YOUR PERCEPTION AS WELL AS YOUR HAND STRENGTH AND CONTROL.

WHEN YOU'VE COPIED THE IMAGE, GO AHEAD AND COLOR IT NEXT! WE'RE EXCITED TO SEE WHAT YOU CAN DO!

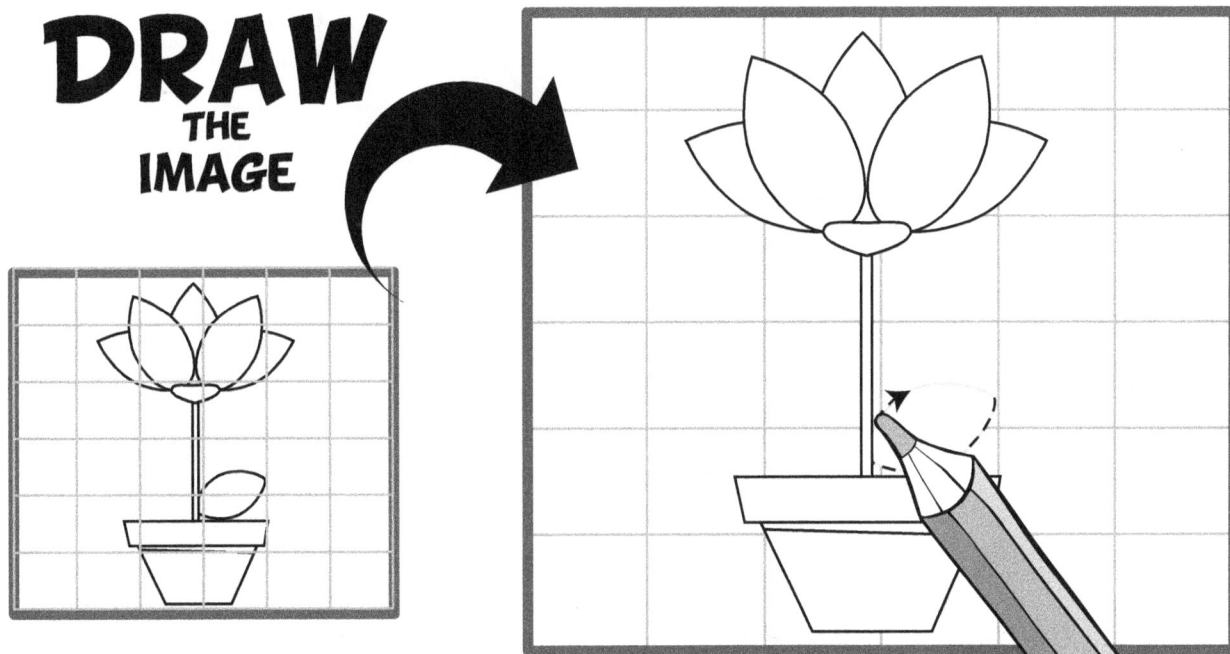

DRAW THE IMAGE

DRAW
THE
DOODLE
IMAGE

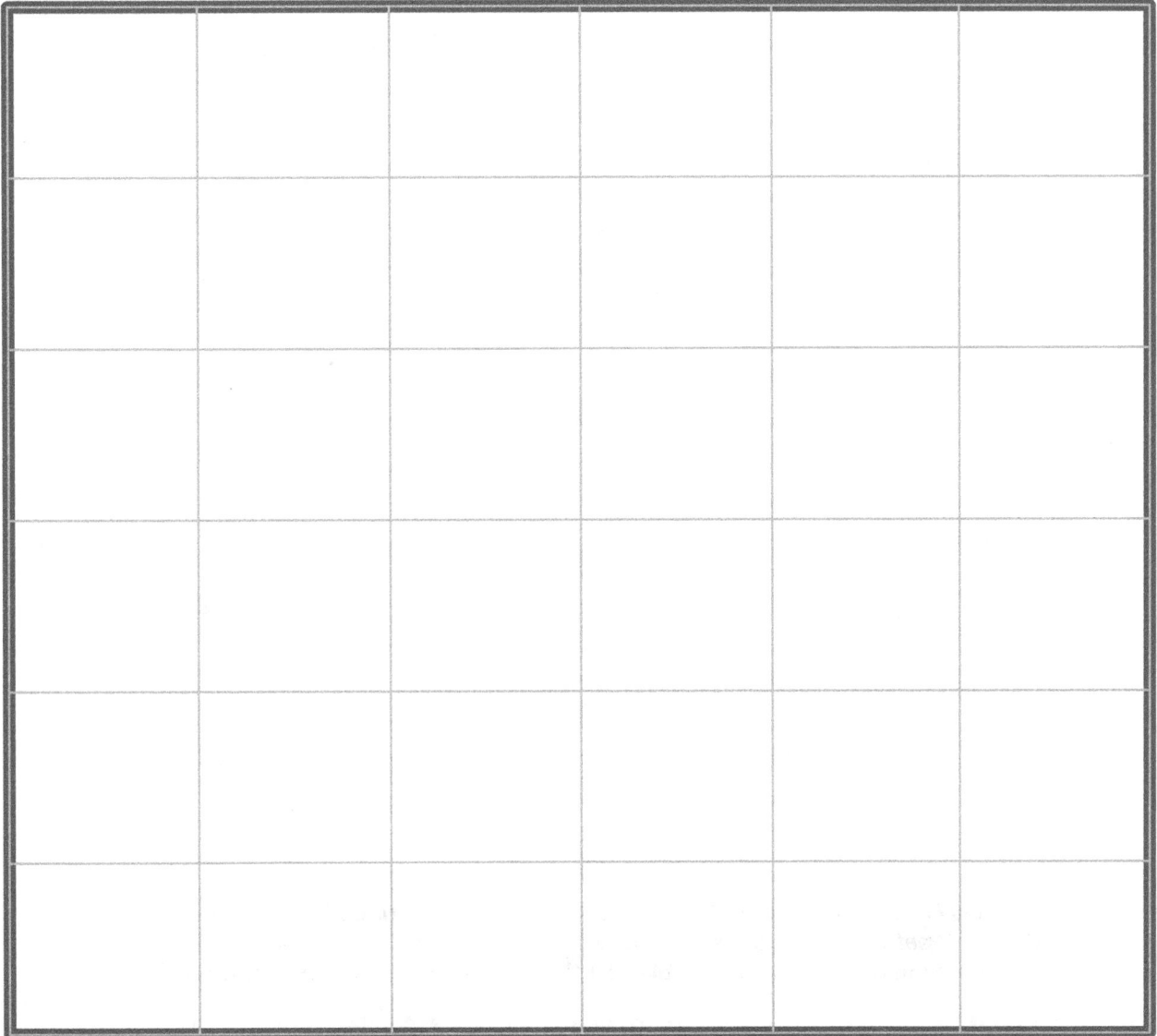

DRAW
THE
DOODLE
IMAGE

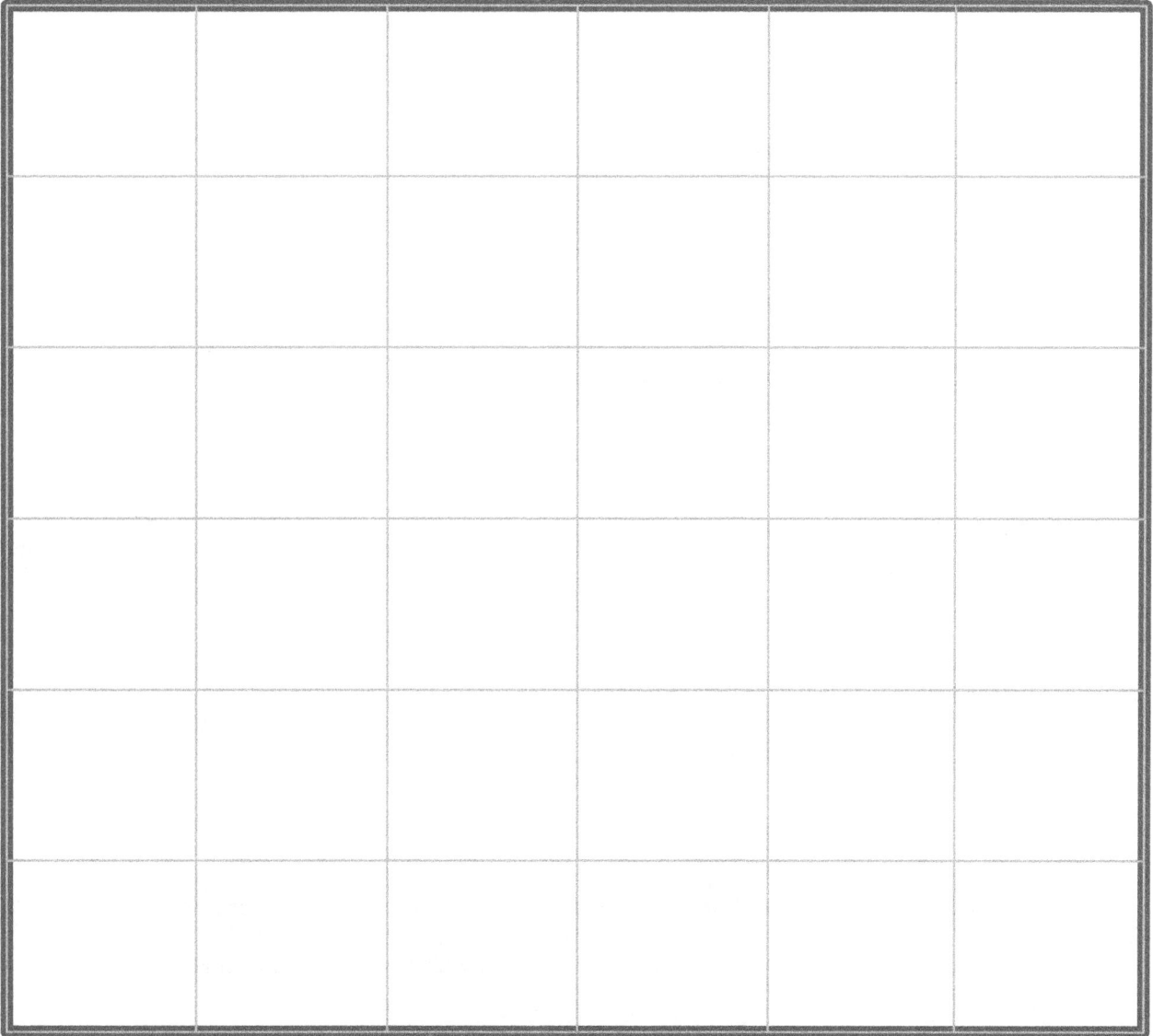

DRAW
THE
DOODLE
IMAGE

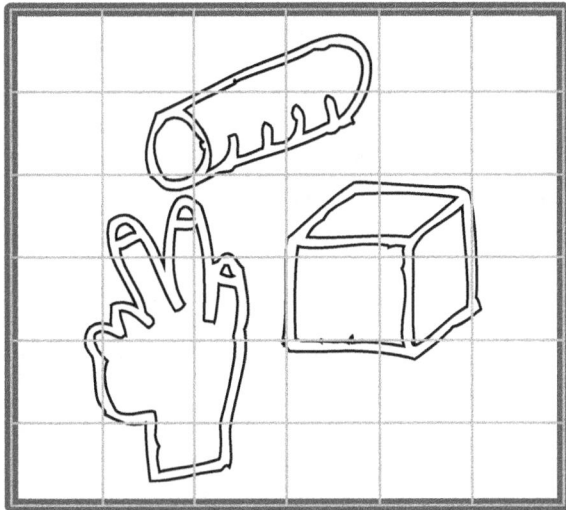

DRAW
THE
DOODLE
IMAGE

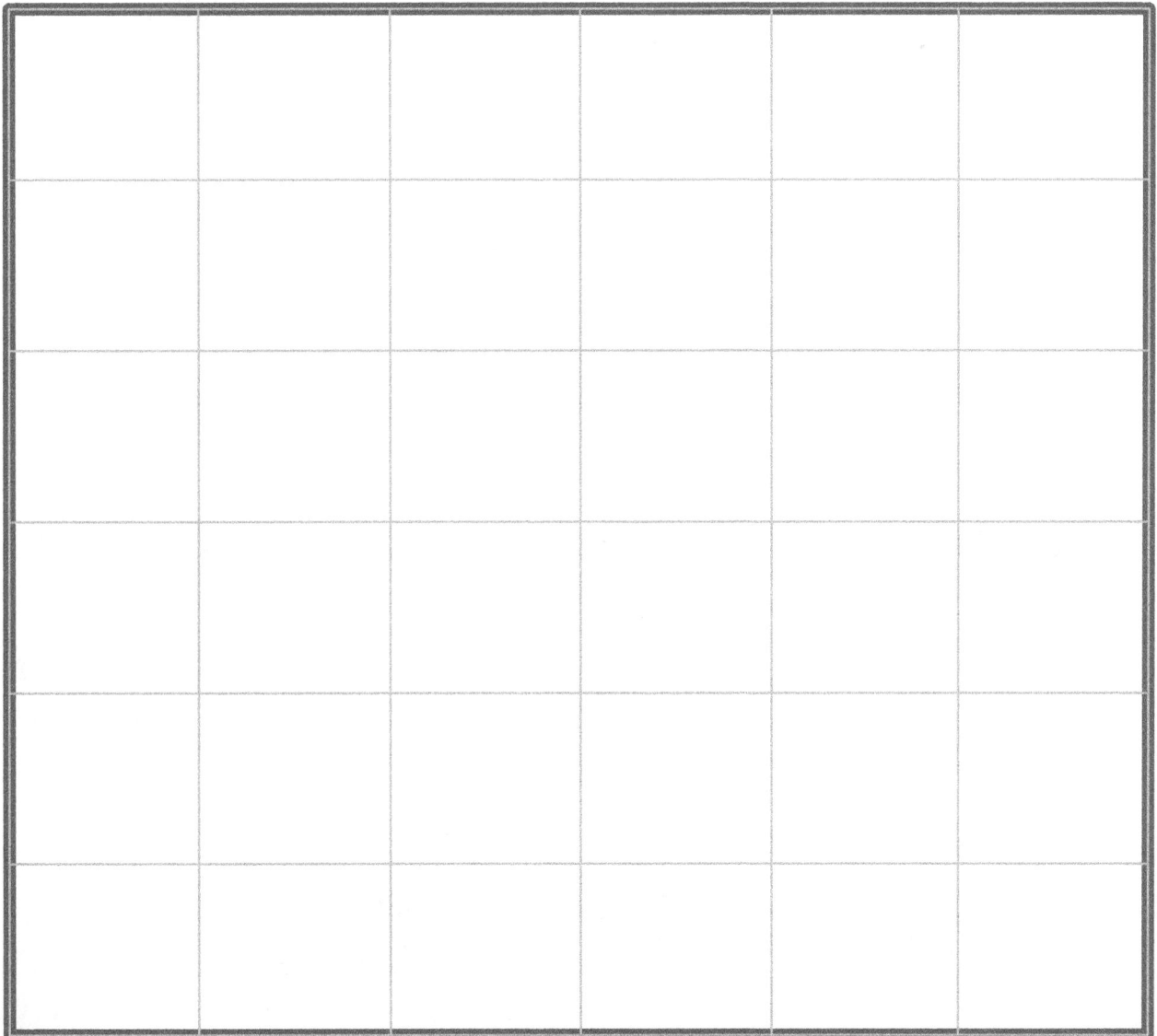

DRAW
THE
DOODLE
IMAGE

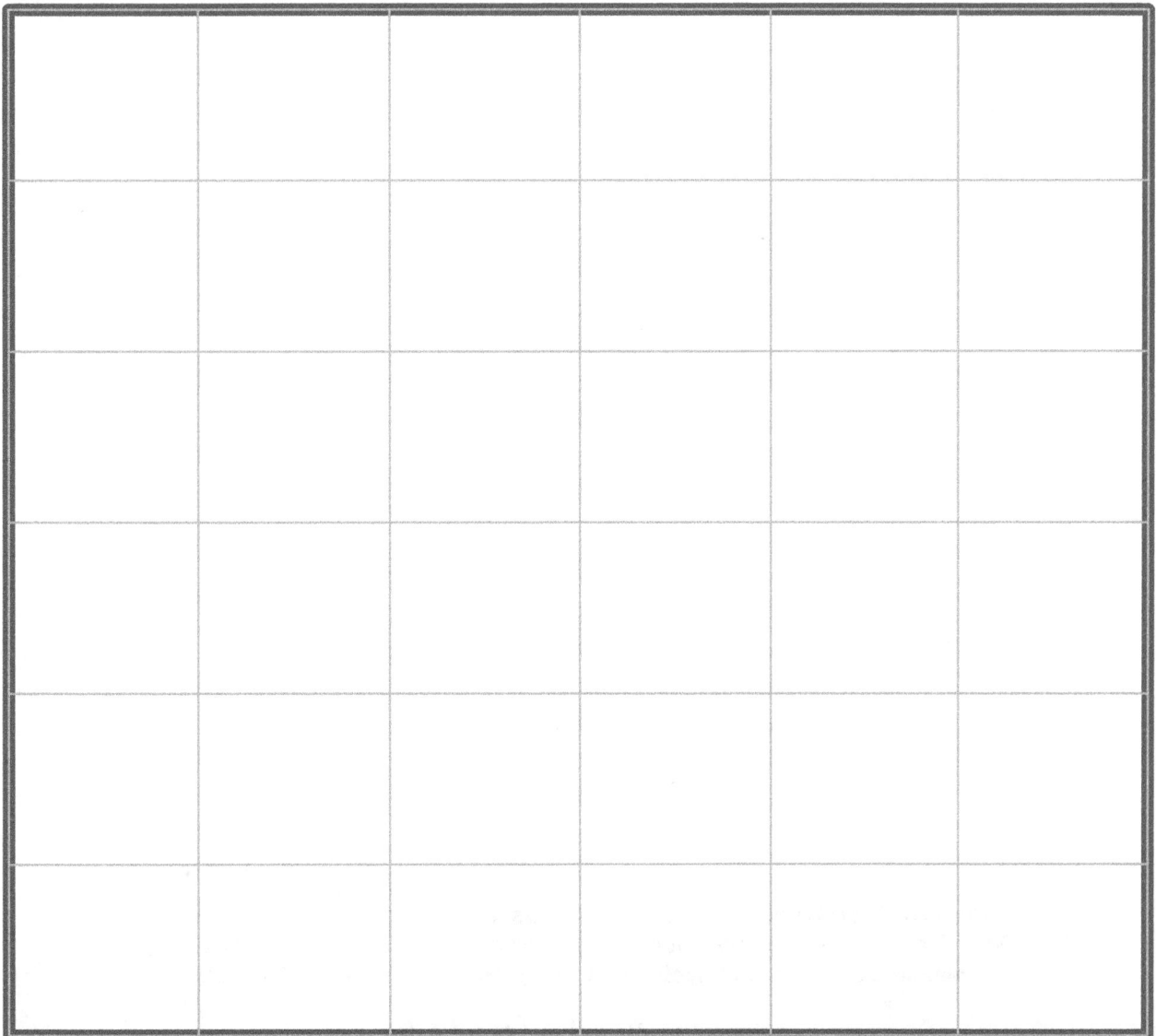

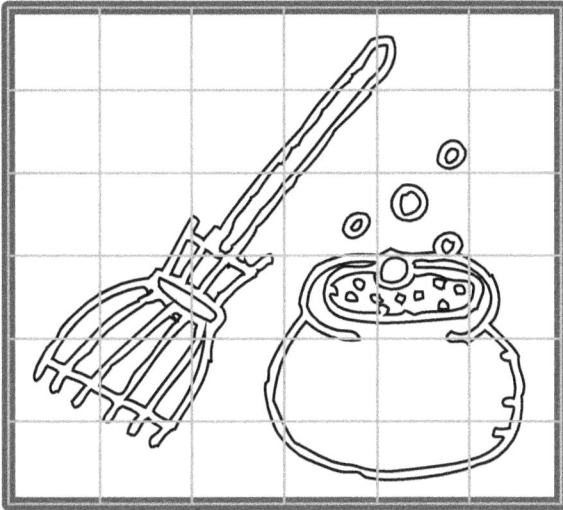

DRAW
THE
DOODLE
IMAGE

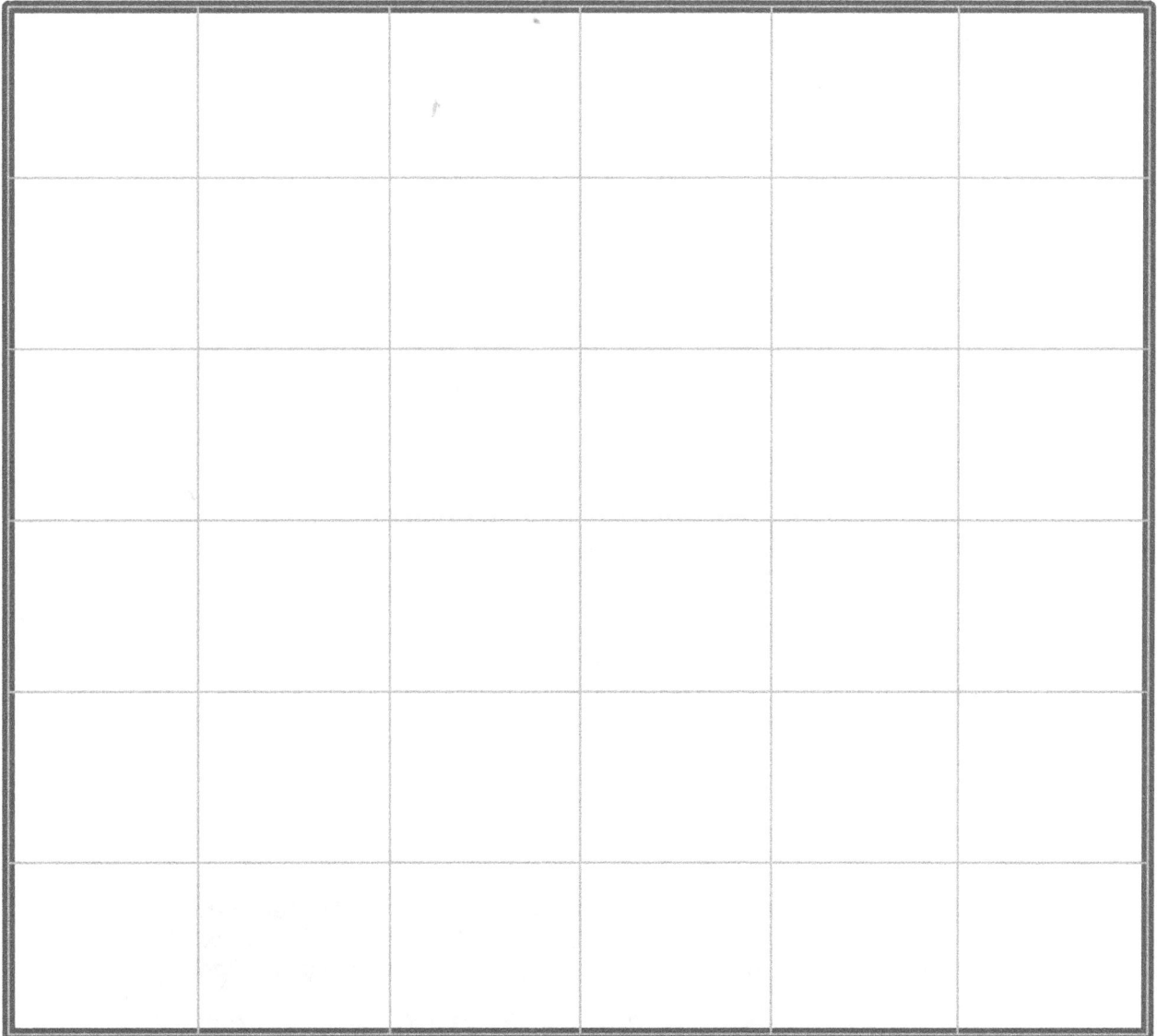

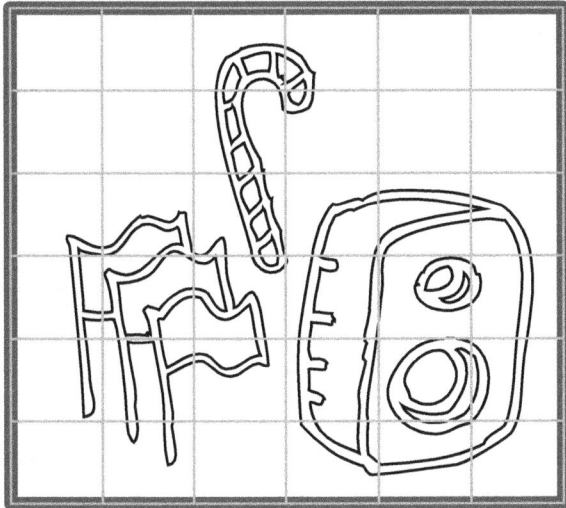

DRAW
THE
DOODLE
IMAGE

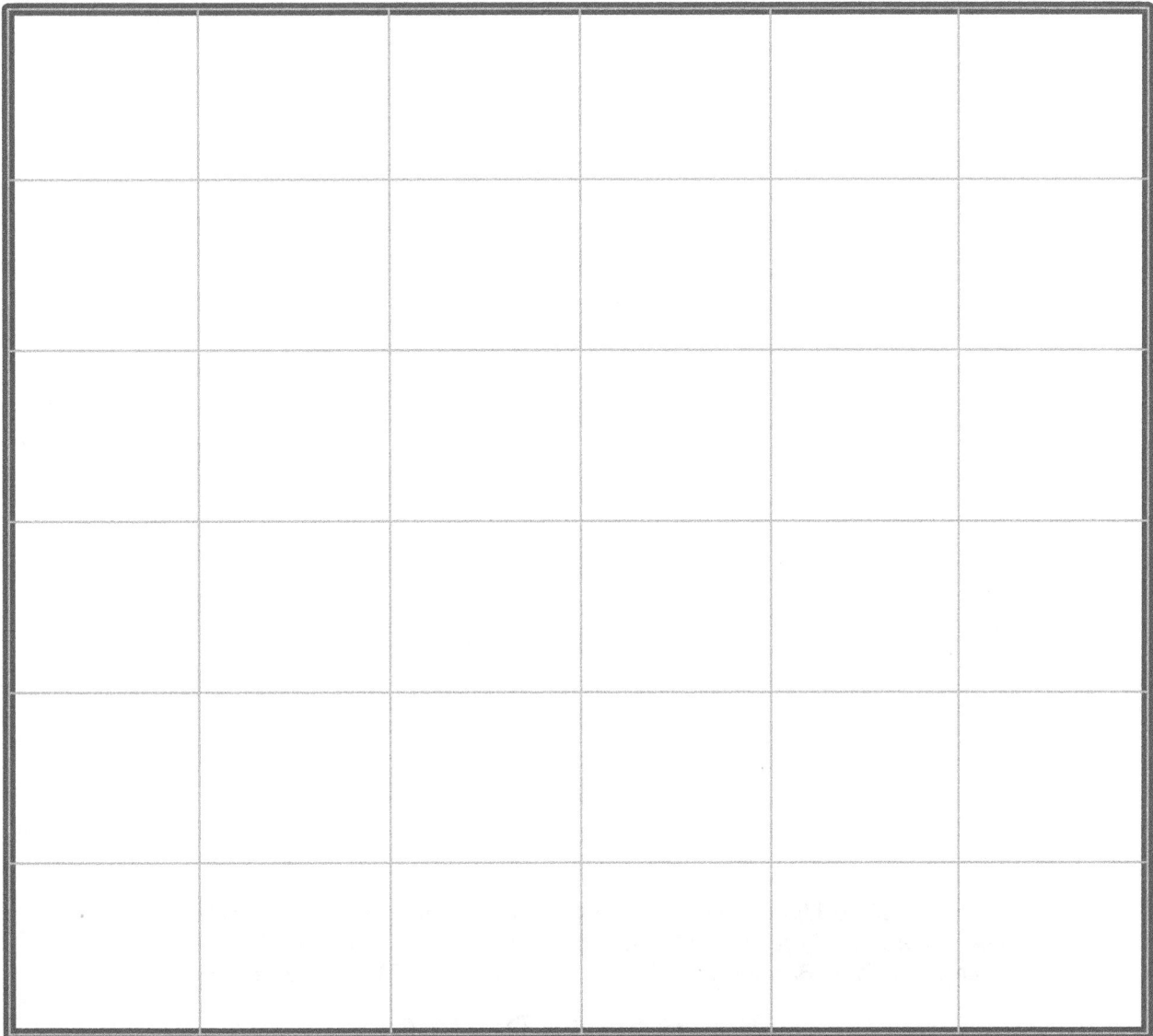

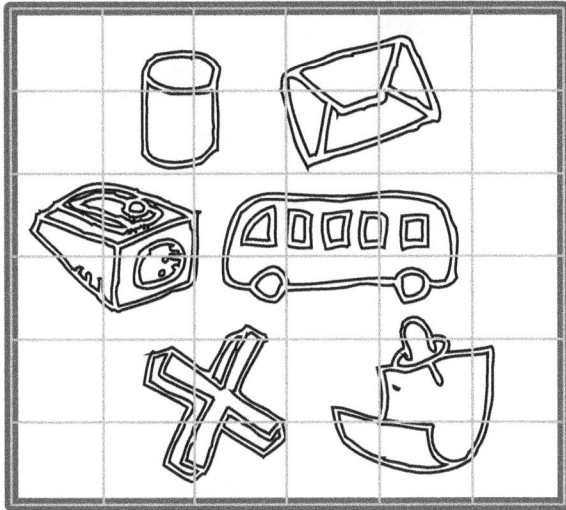

DRAW
THE
IMAGE

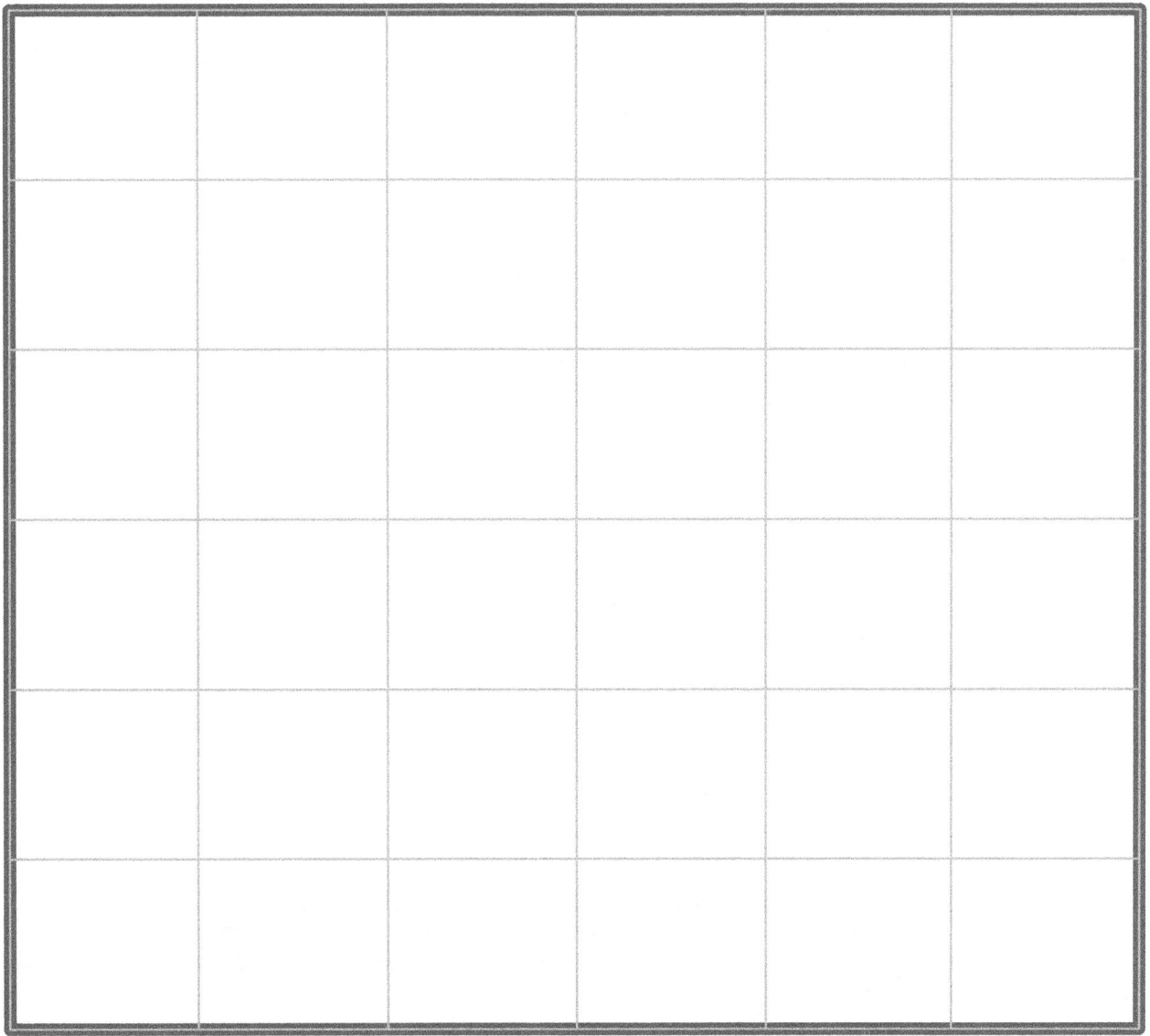

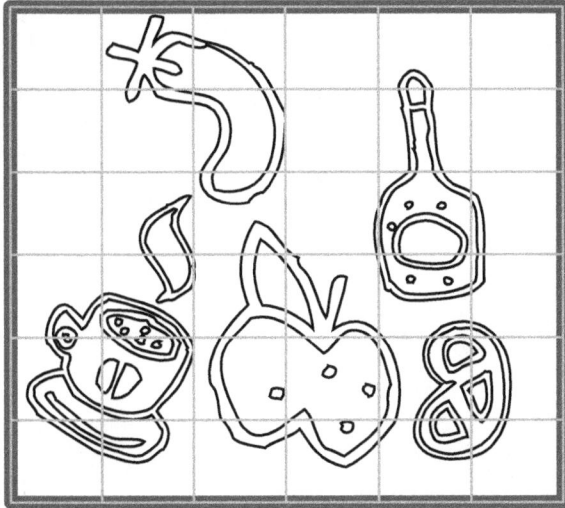

DRAW
THE
IMAGE

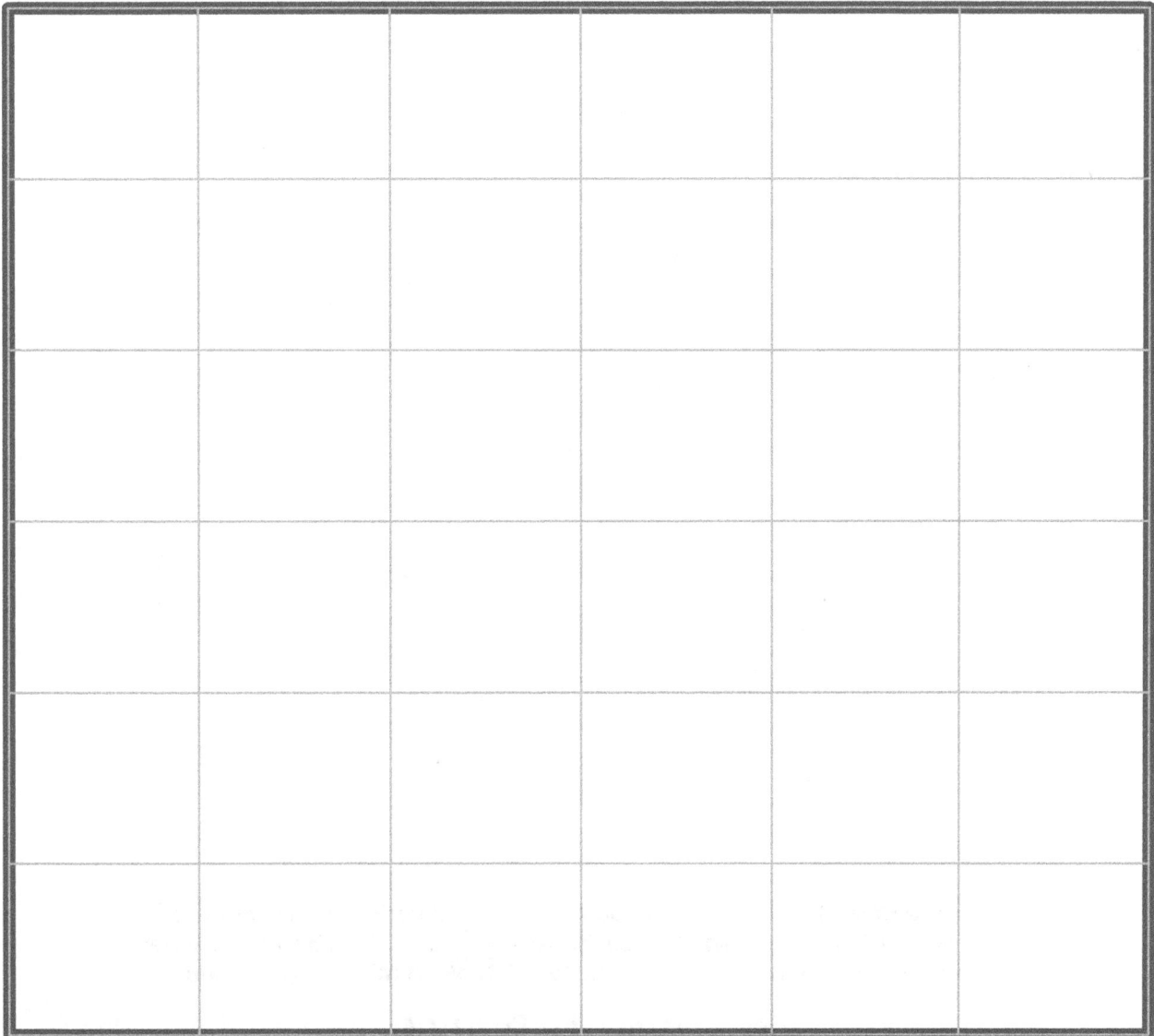

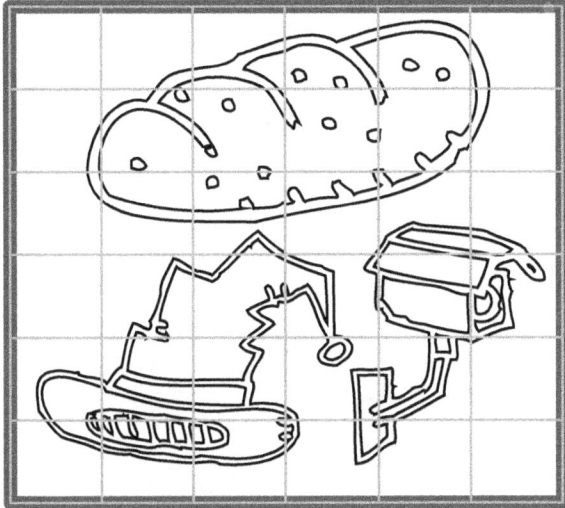

DRAW
THE
DOODLE
IMAGE

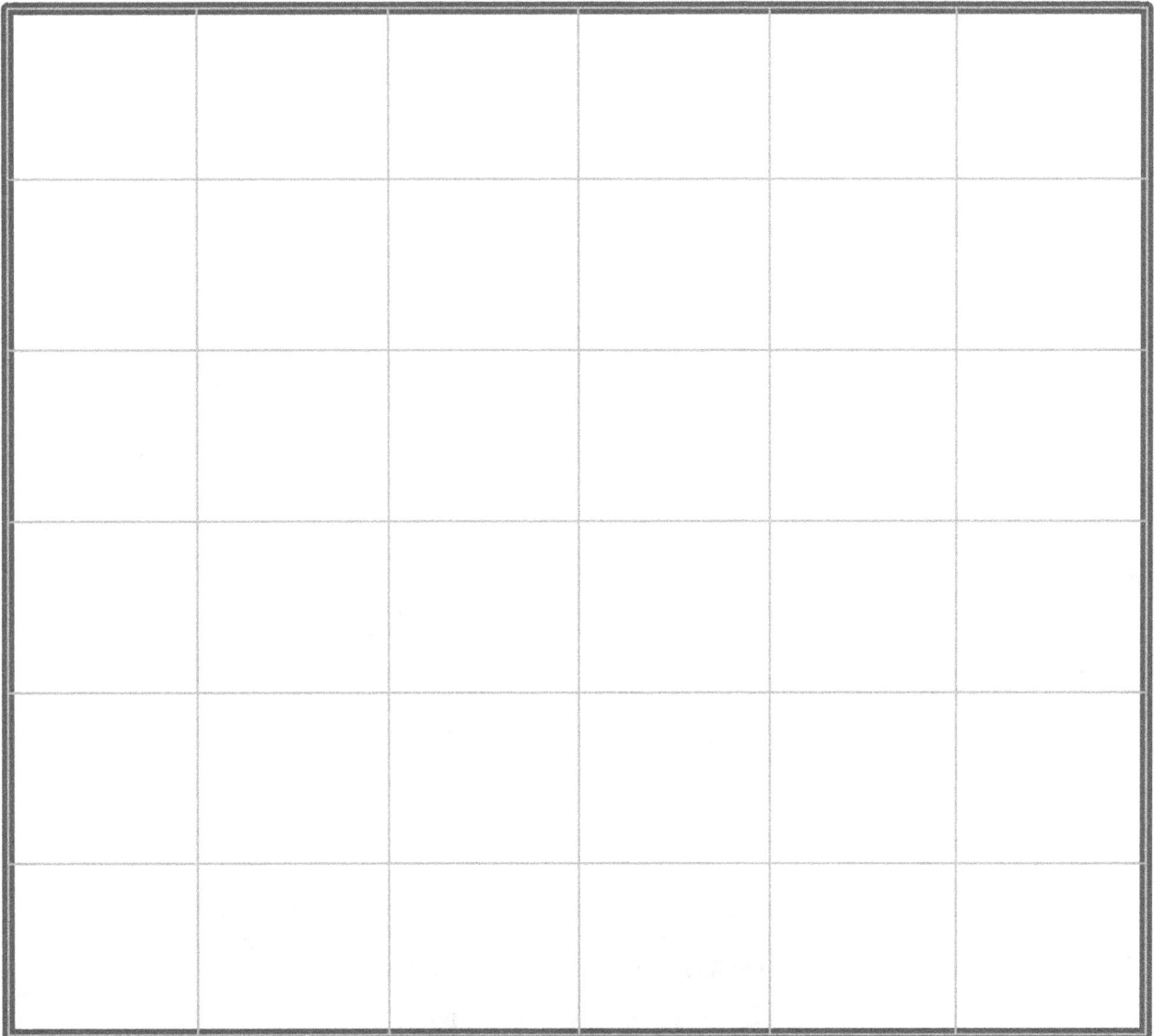

DRAW
THE
DOODLE
IMAGE

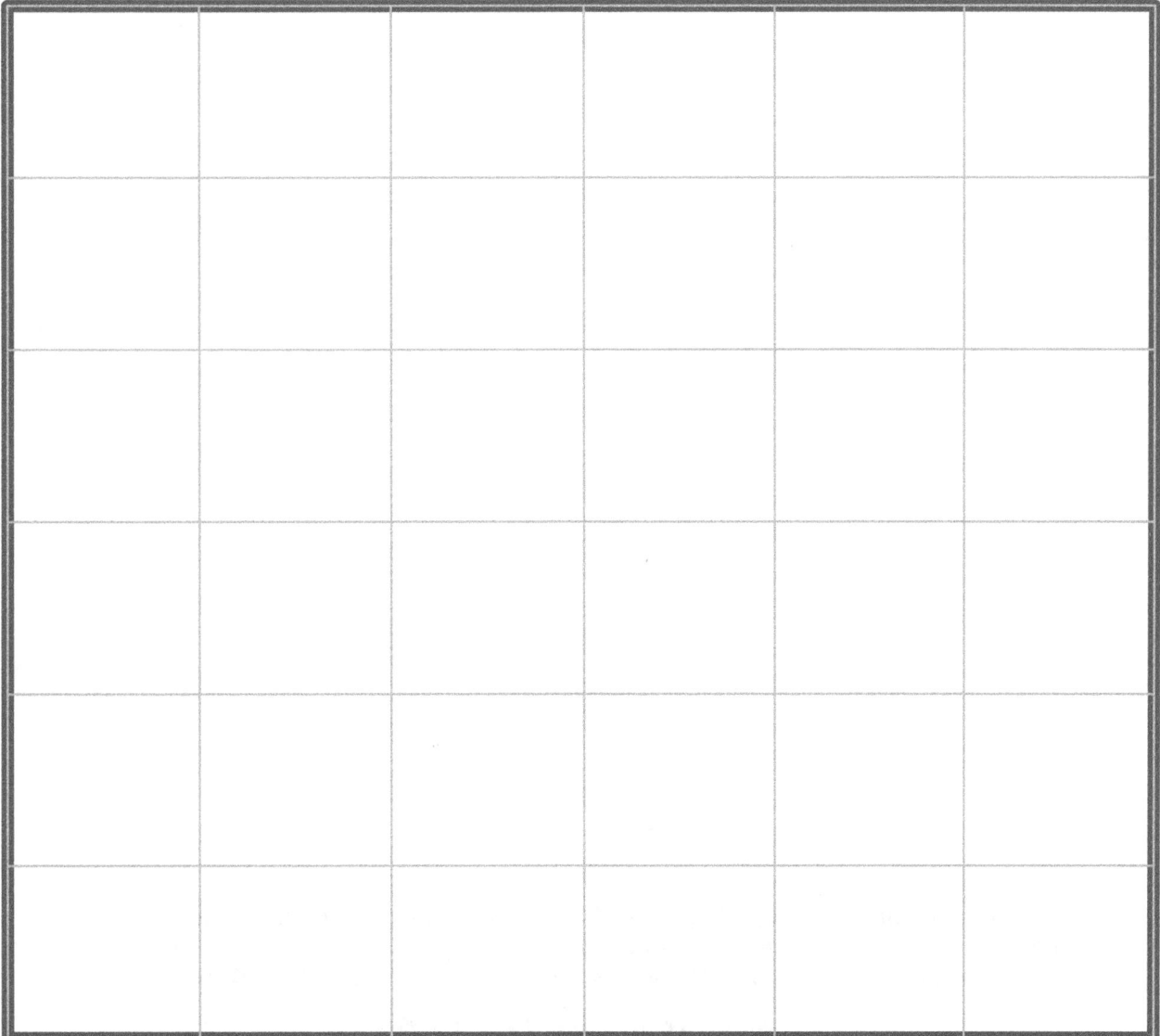

DRAW
THE
DOODLE
IMAGE

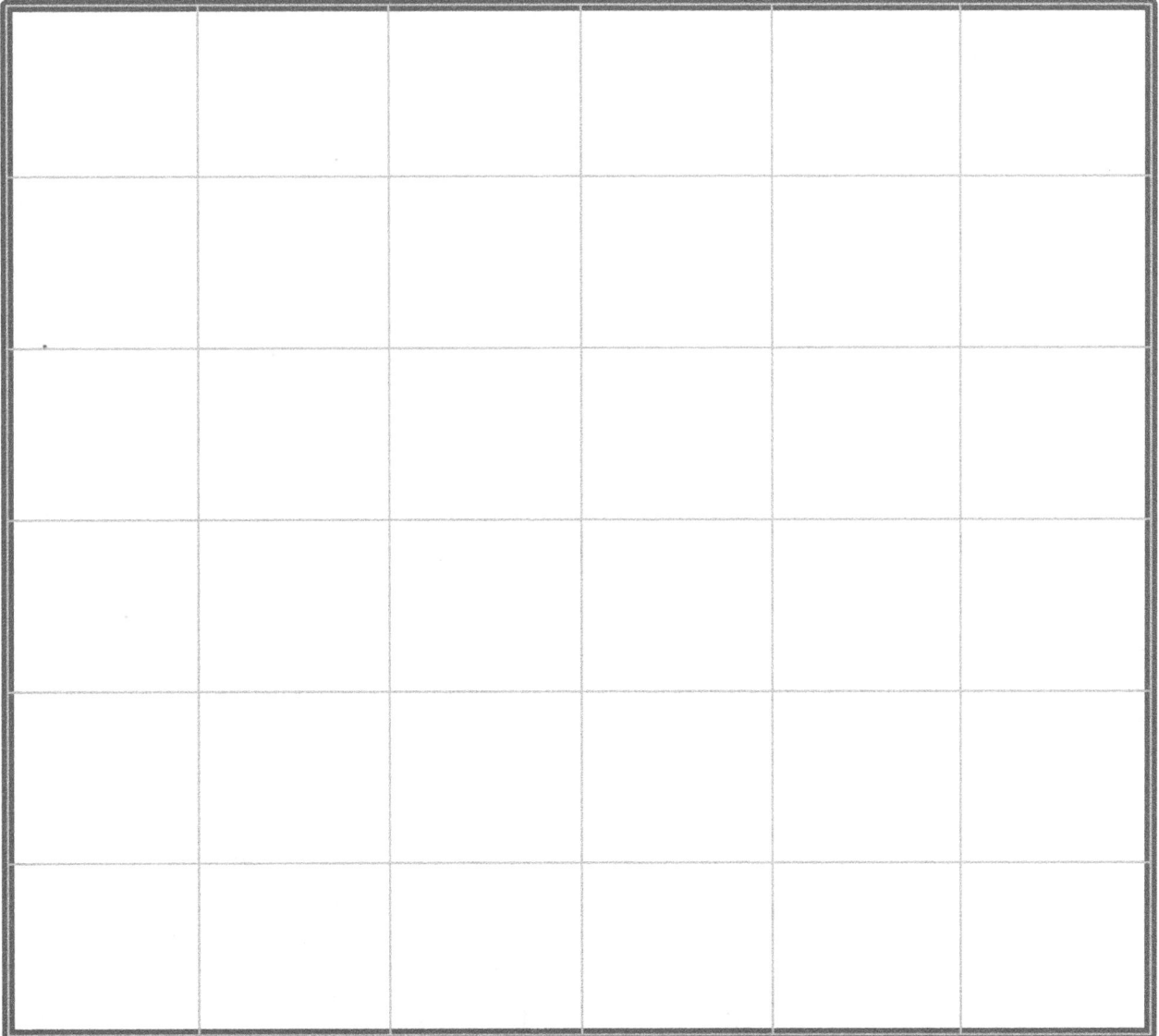

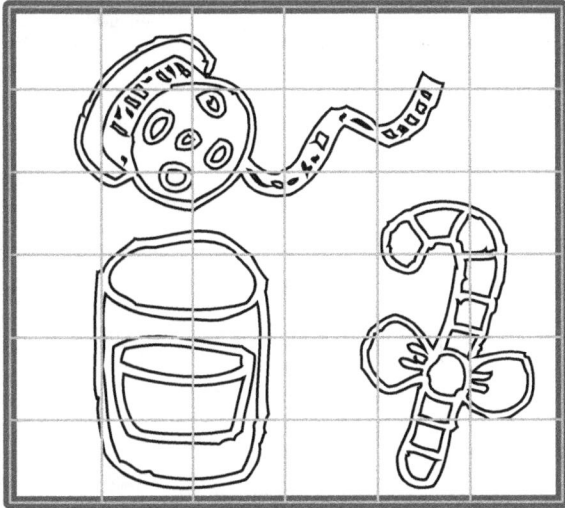

DRAW
THE
DOODLE
IMAGE

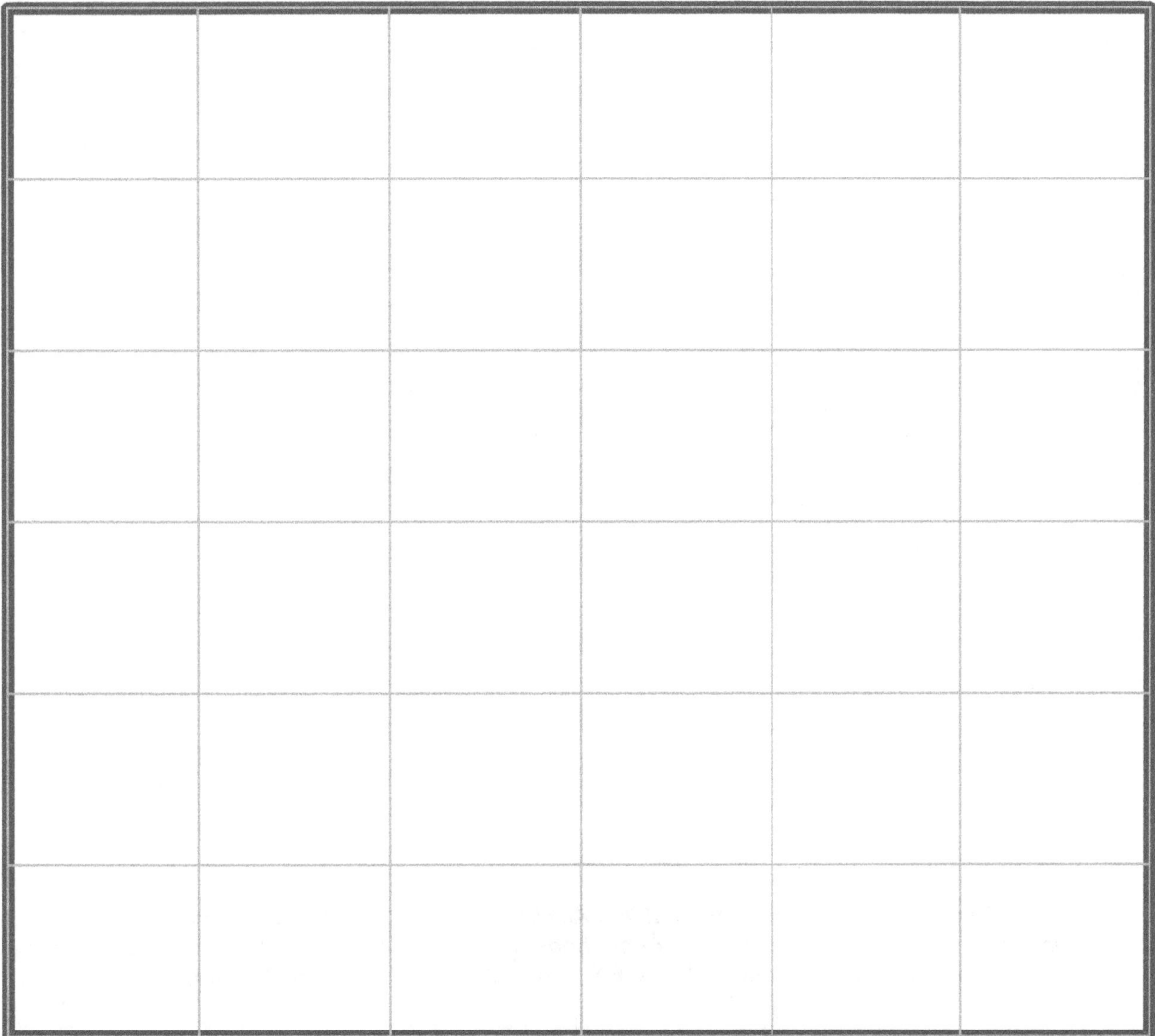

DRAW
THE
DOODLE
IMAGE

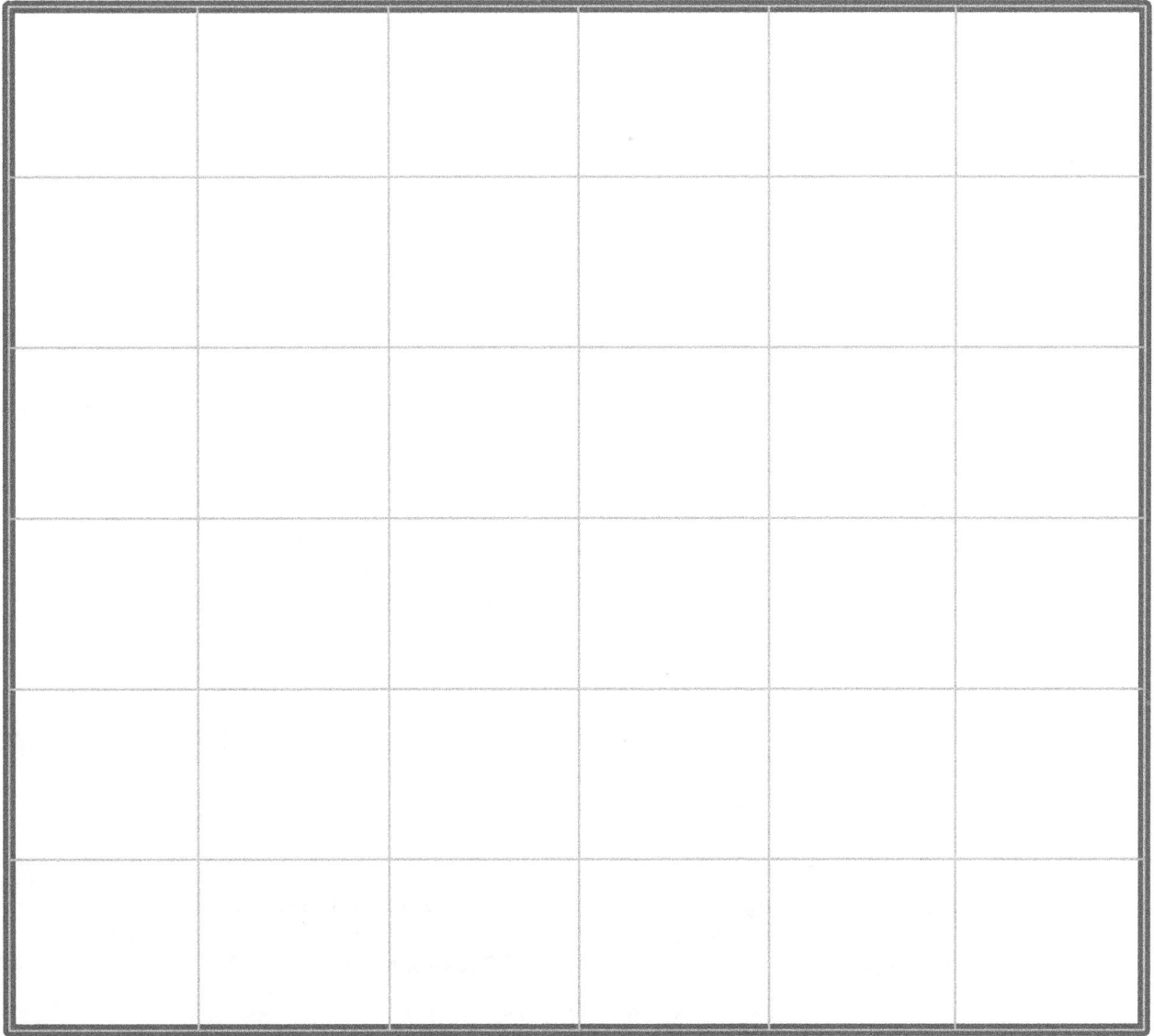

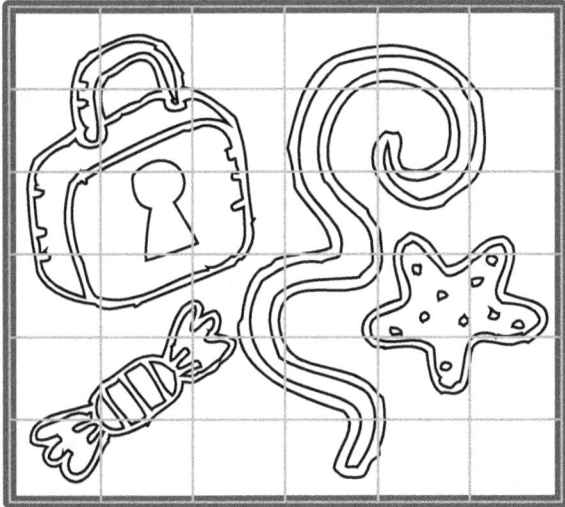

DRAW
THE
DOODLE
IMAGE

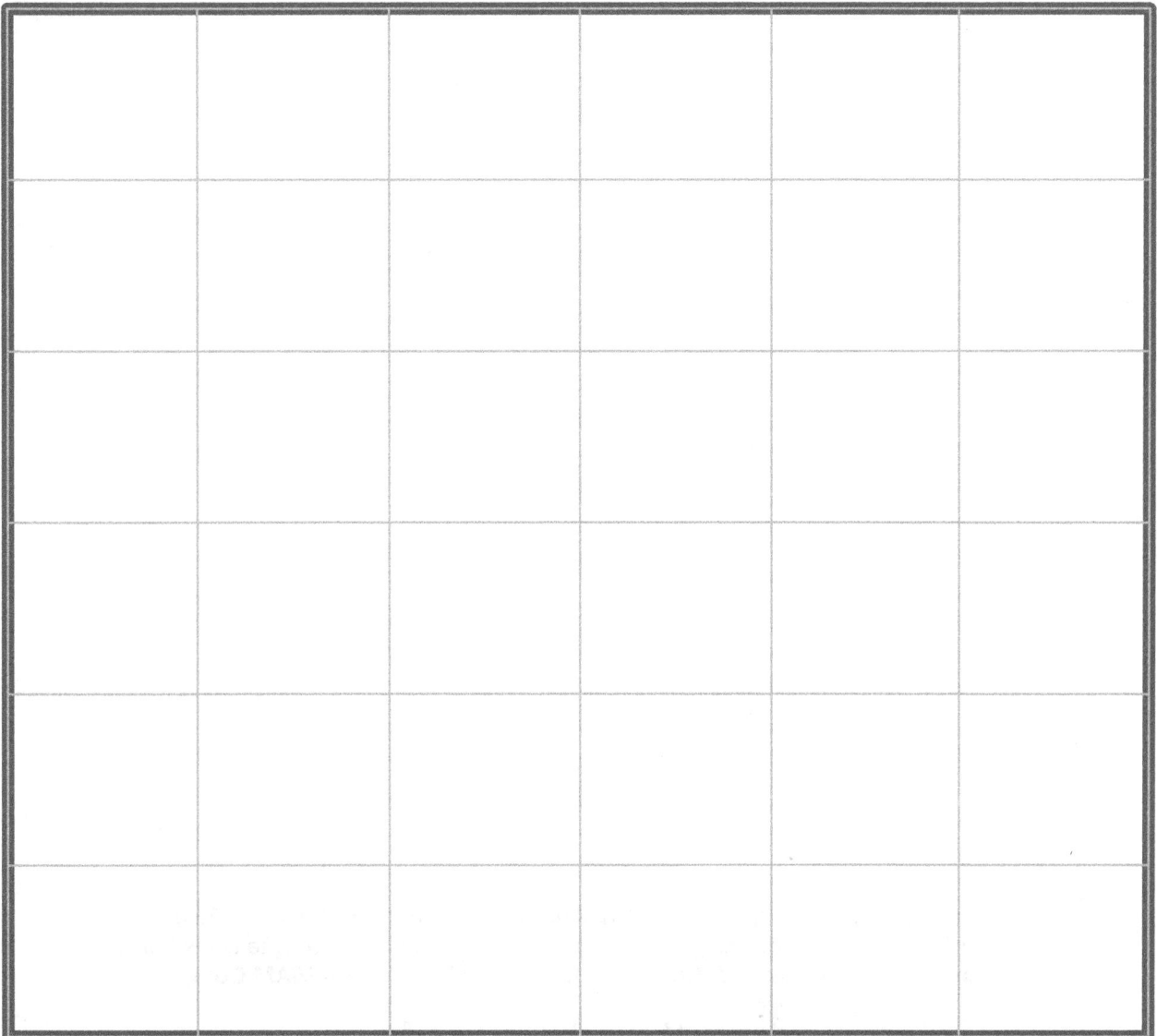

DRAW
THE
DOODLE
IMAGE

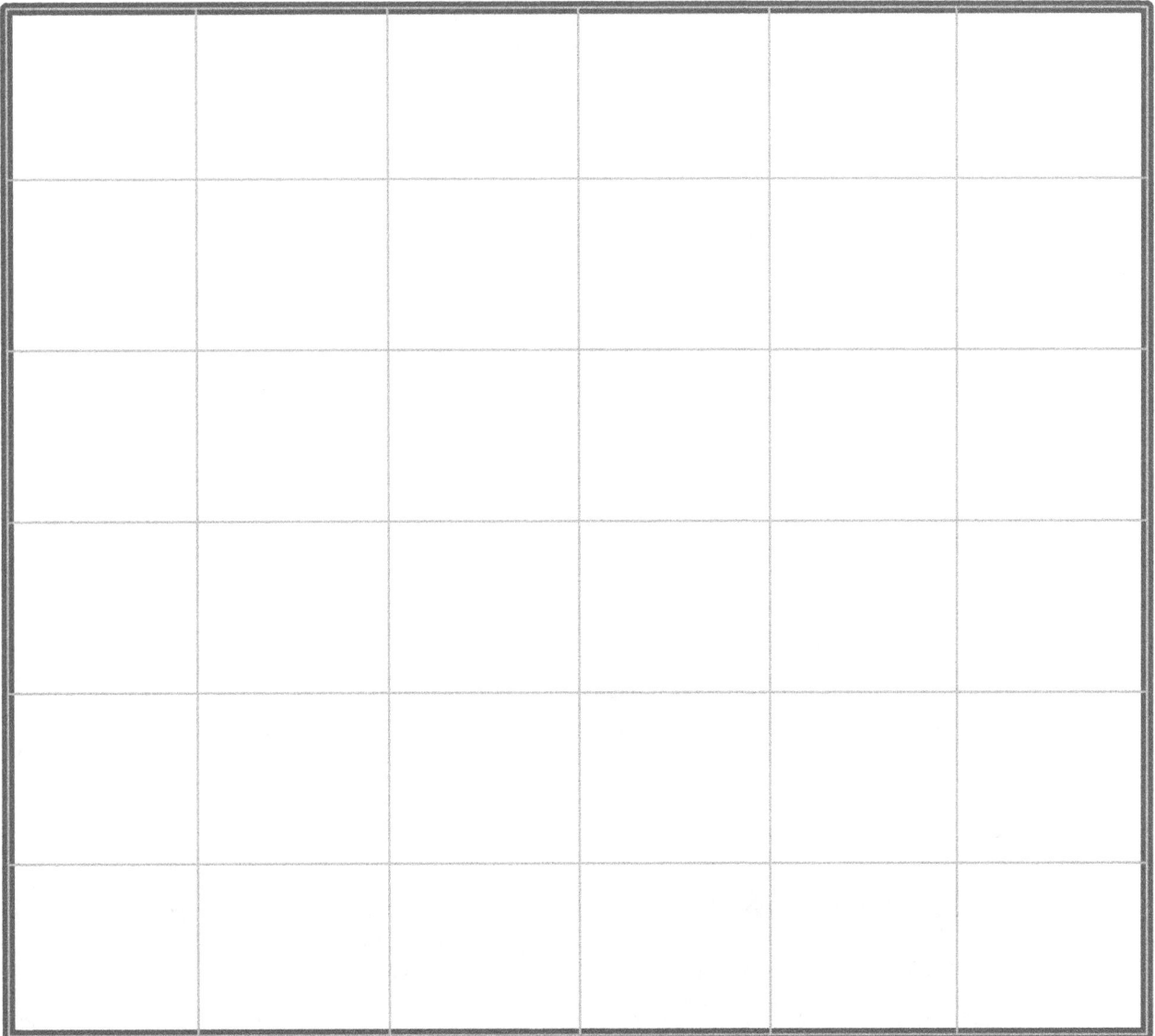

DRAW
THE
DOODLE
IMAGE

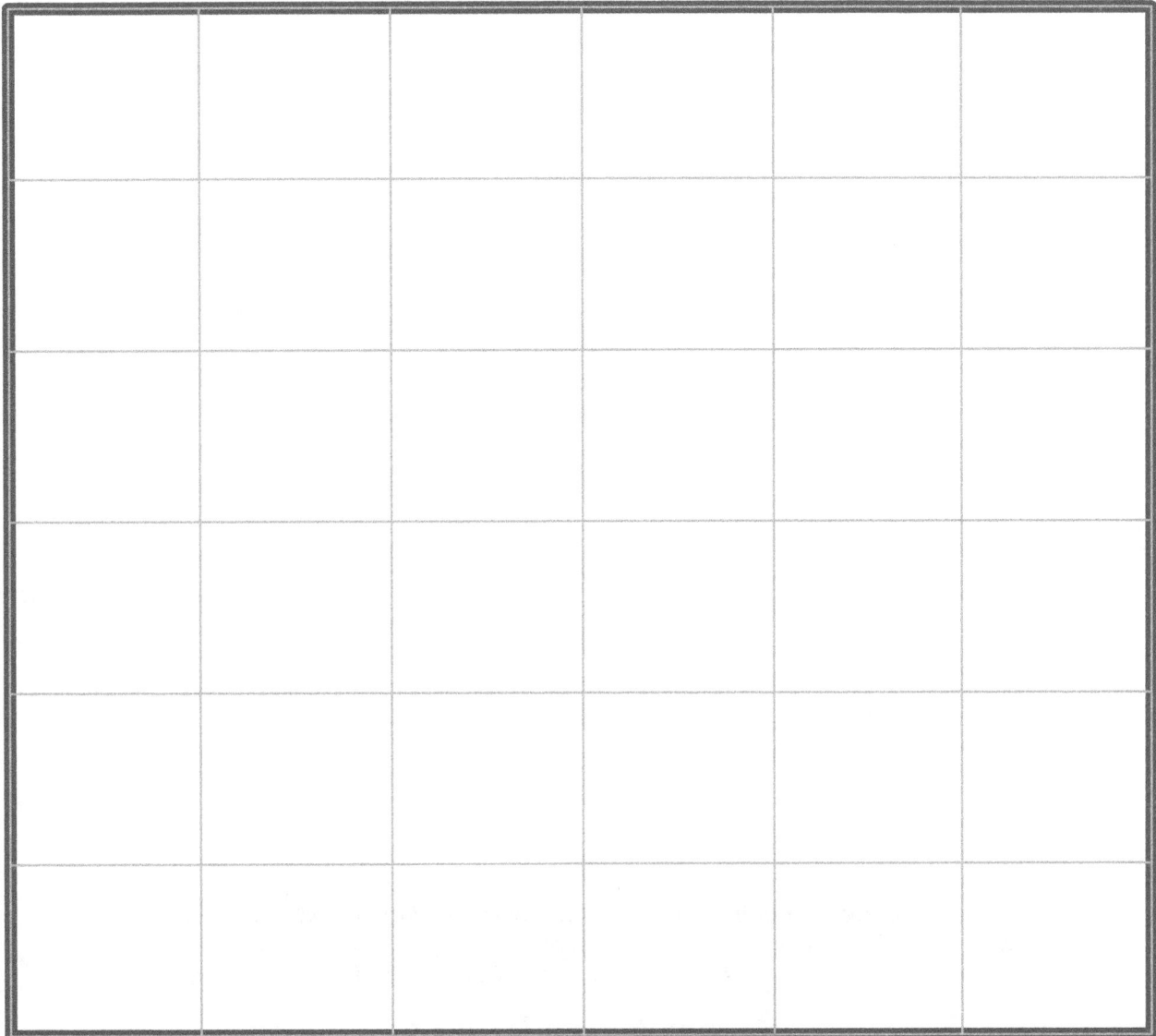

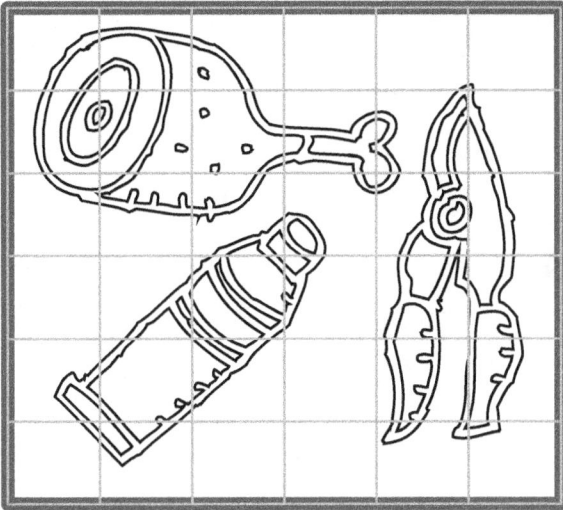

DRAW
THE
DOODLE
IMAGE

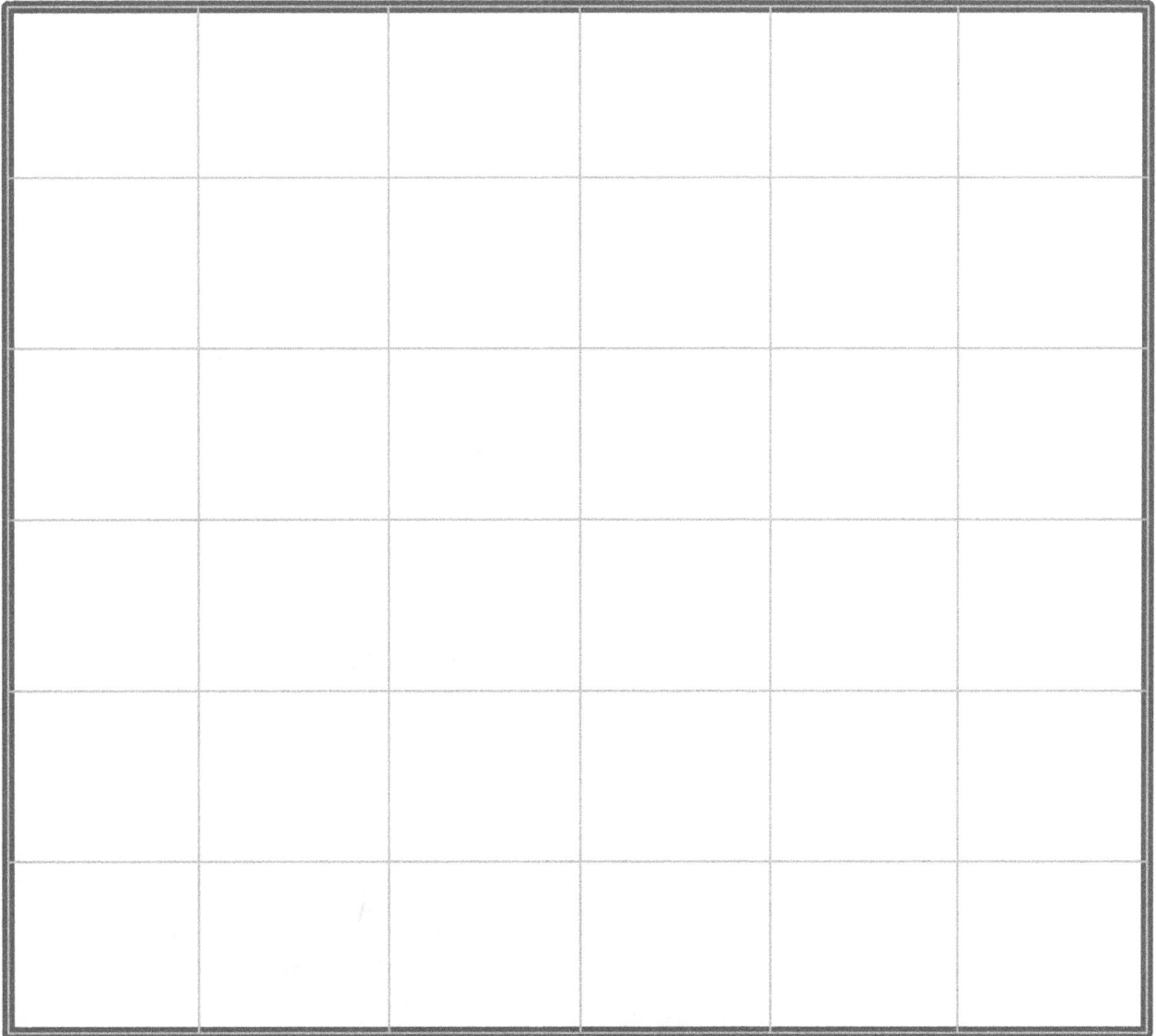

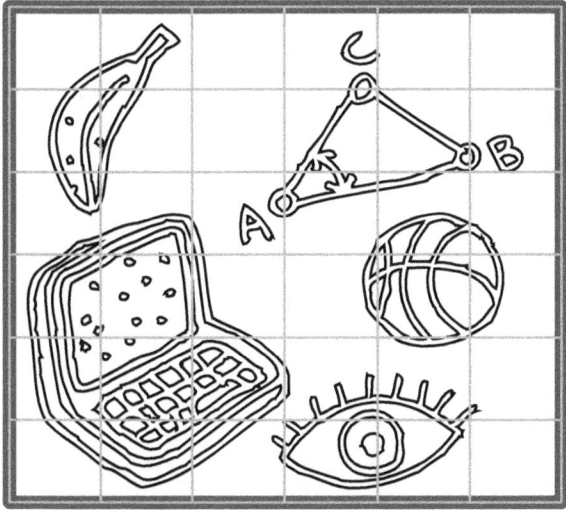

DRAW
THE
IMAGE

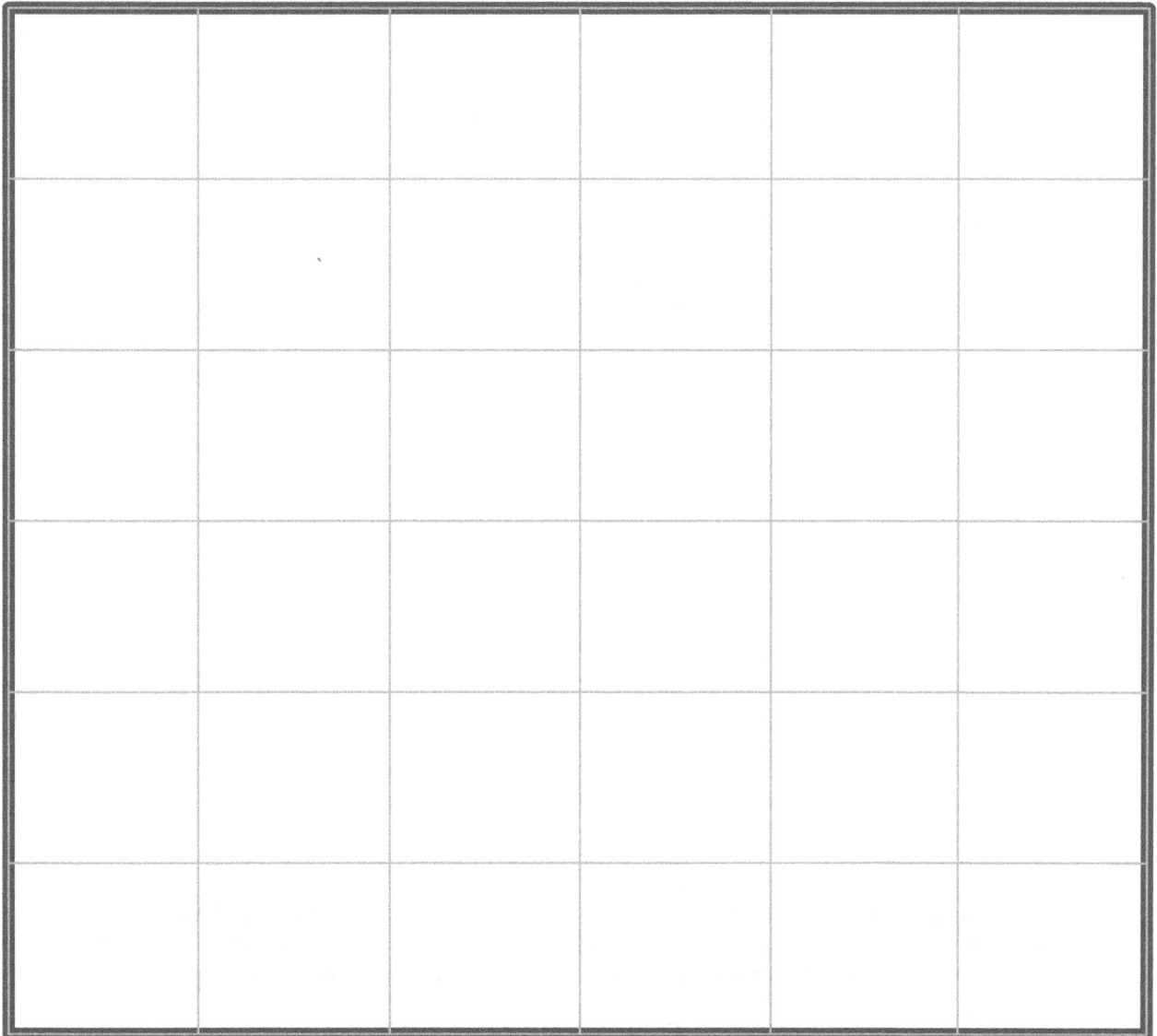

DRAW
THE
IMAGE

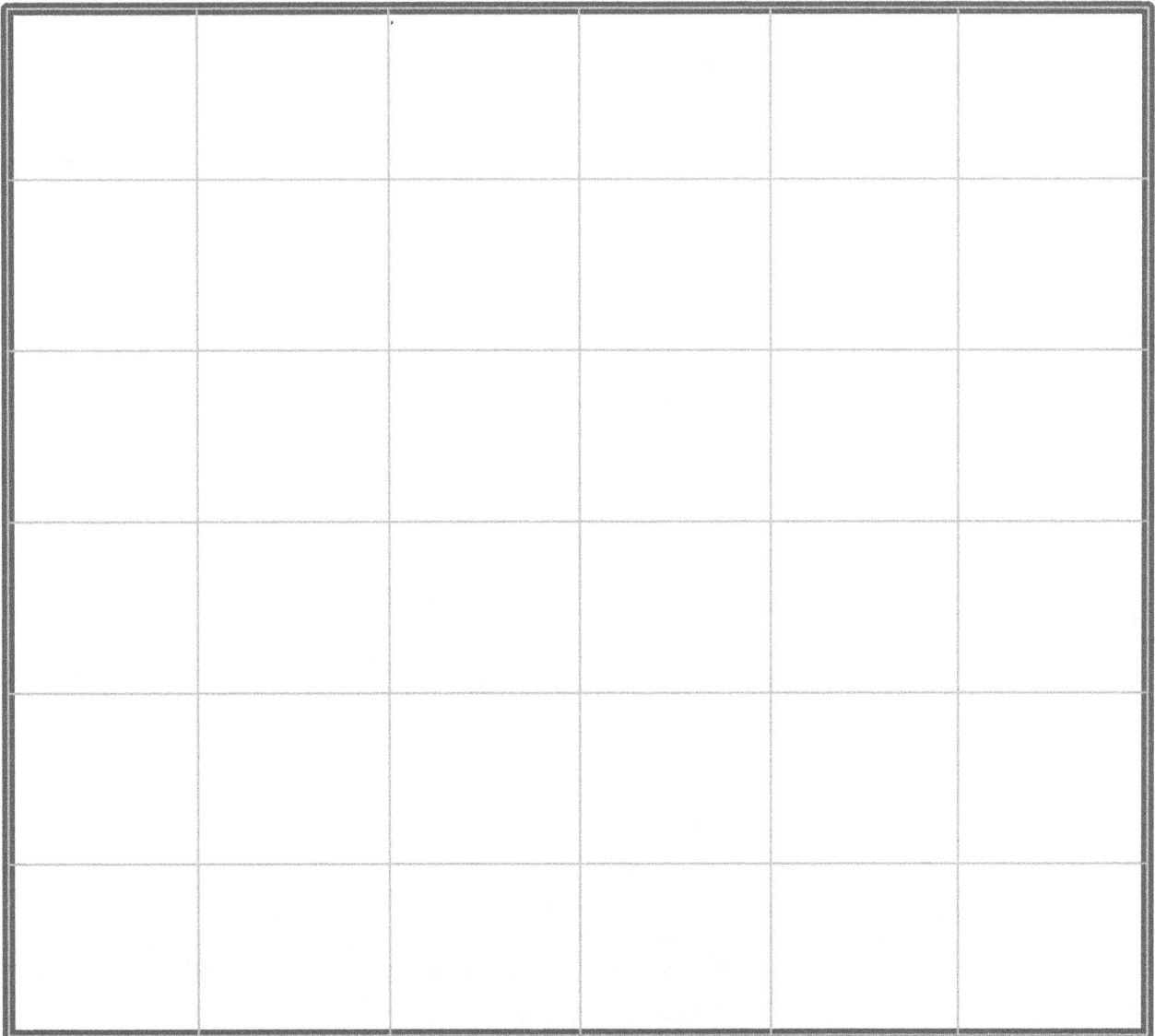

DRAW
THE
IMAGE

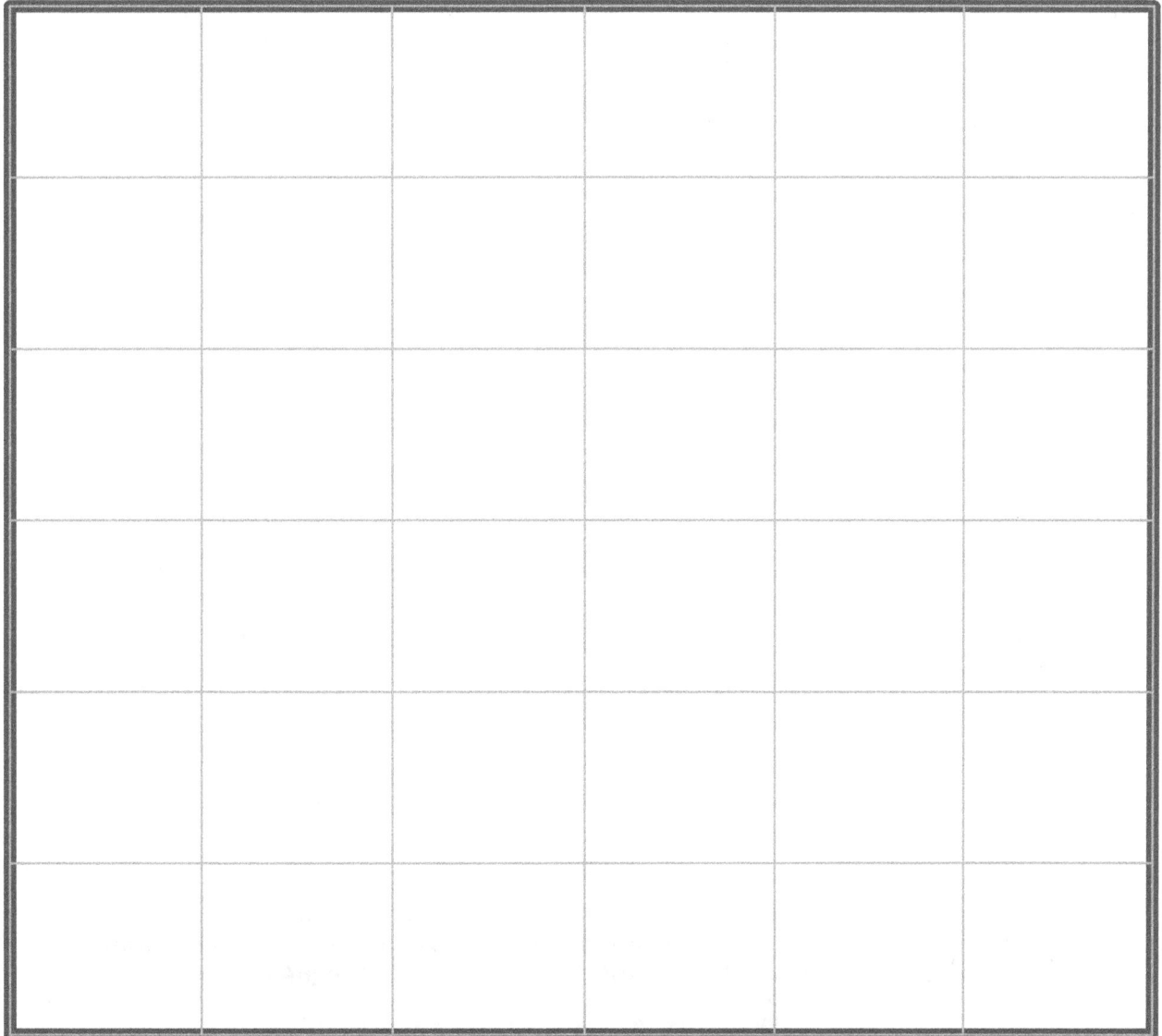

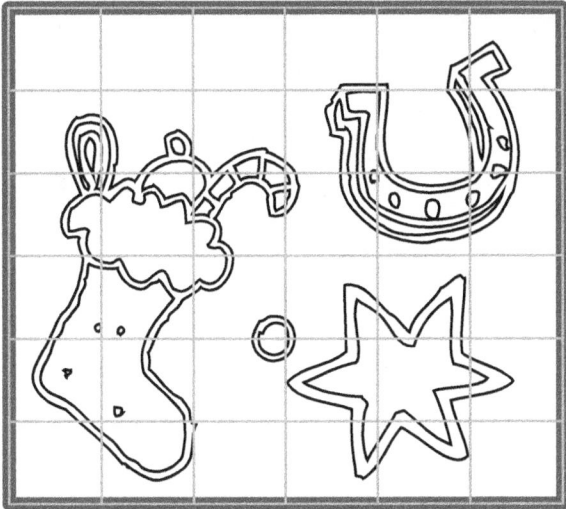

DRAW
THE
DOODLE
IMAGE

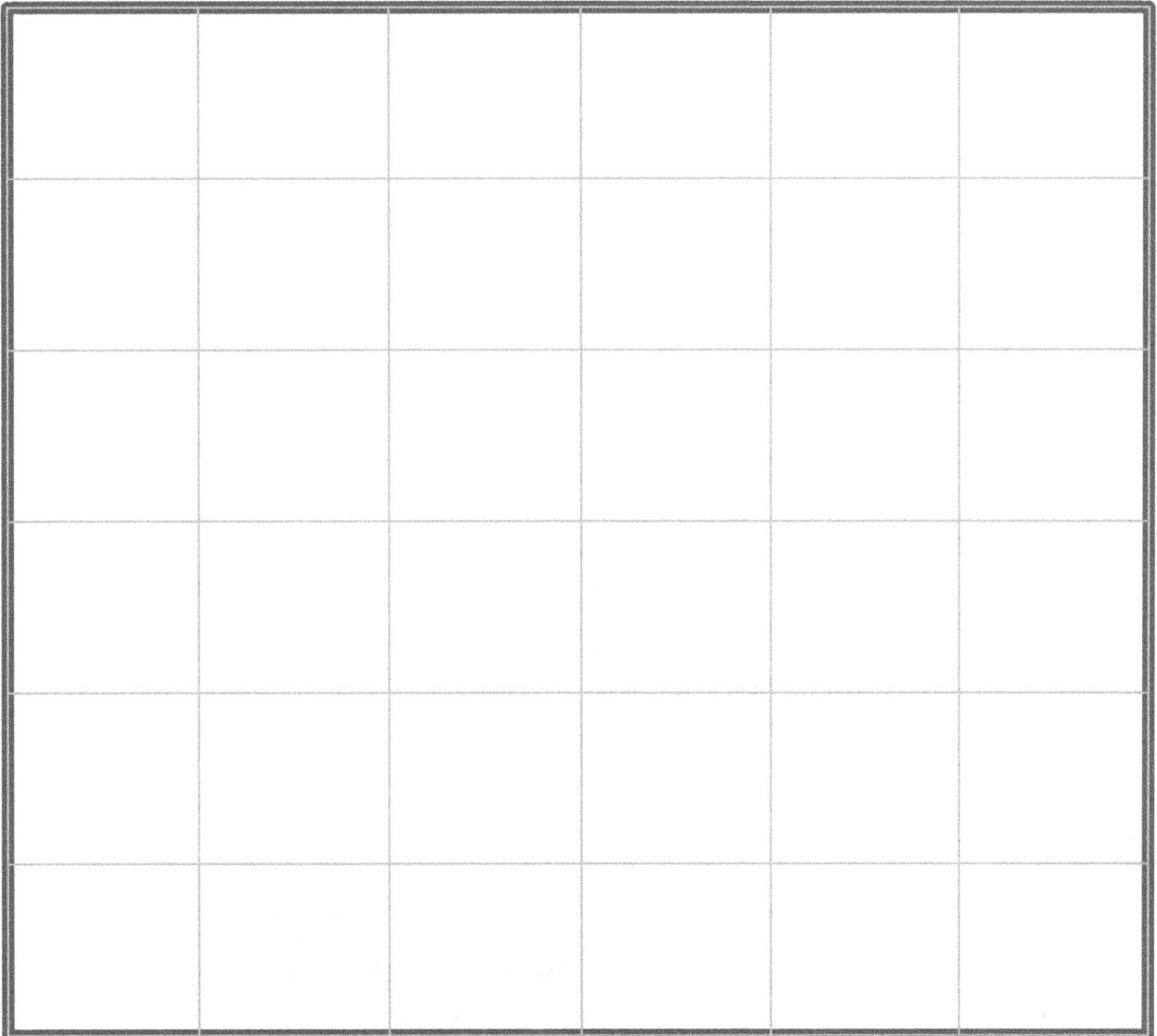

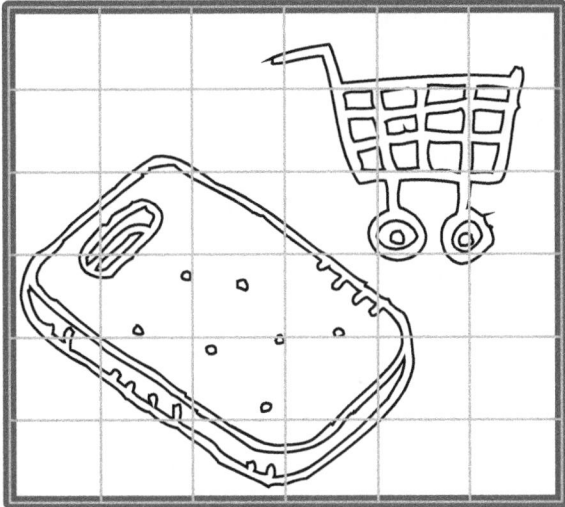

DRAW
THE
DOODLE
IMAGE

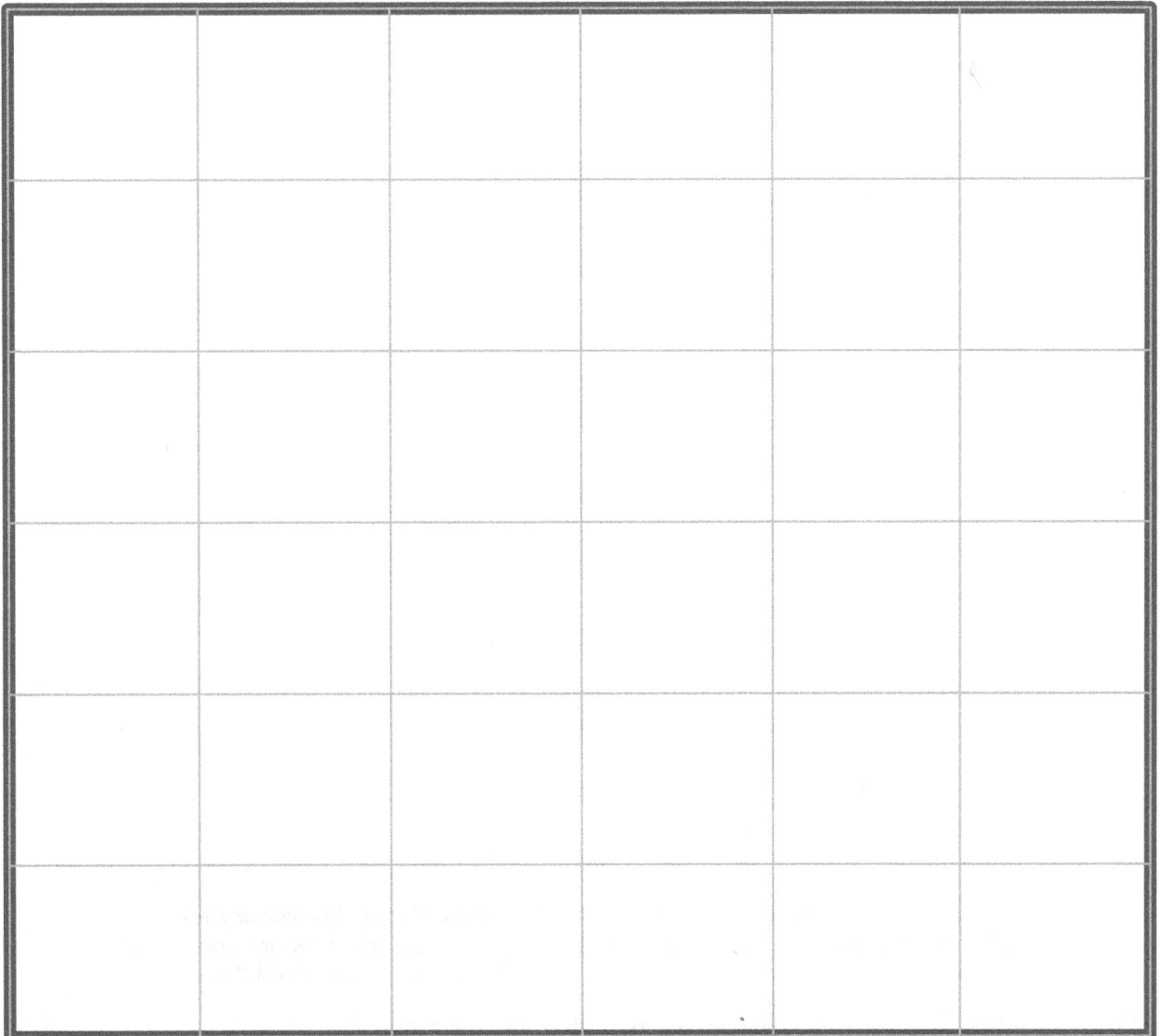

DRAW
THE
DOODLE
IMAGE

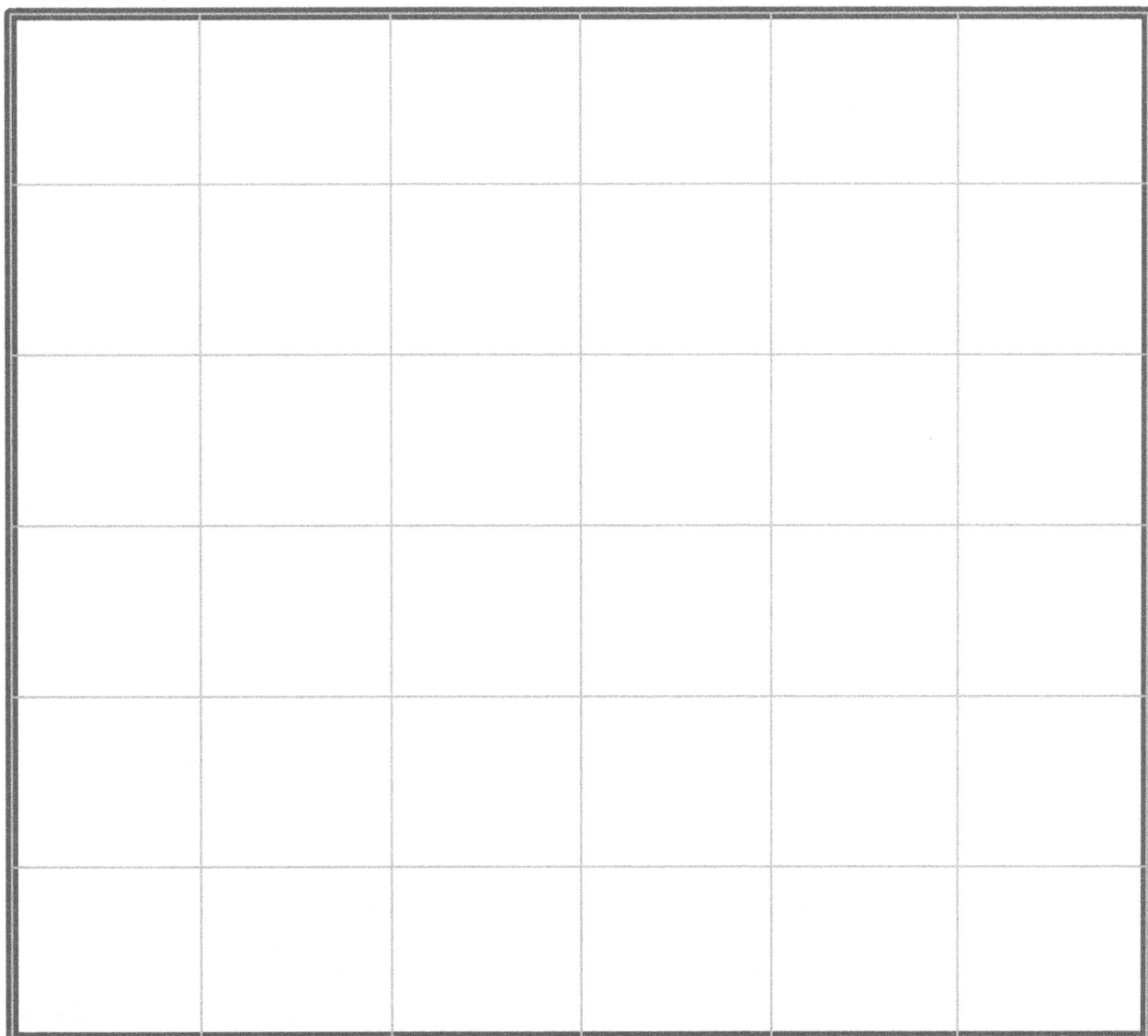

DRAW
THE
IMAGE

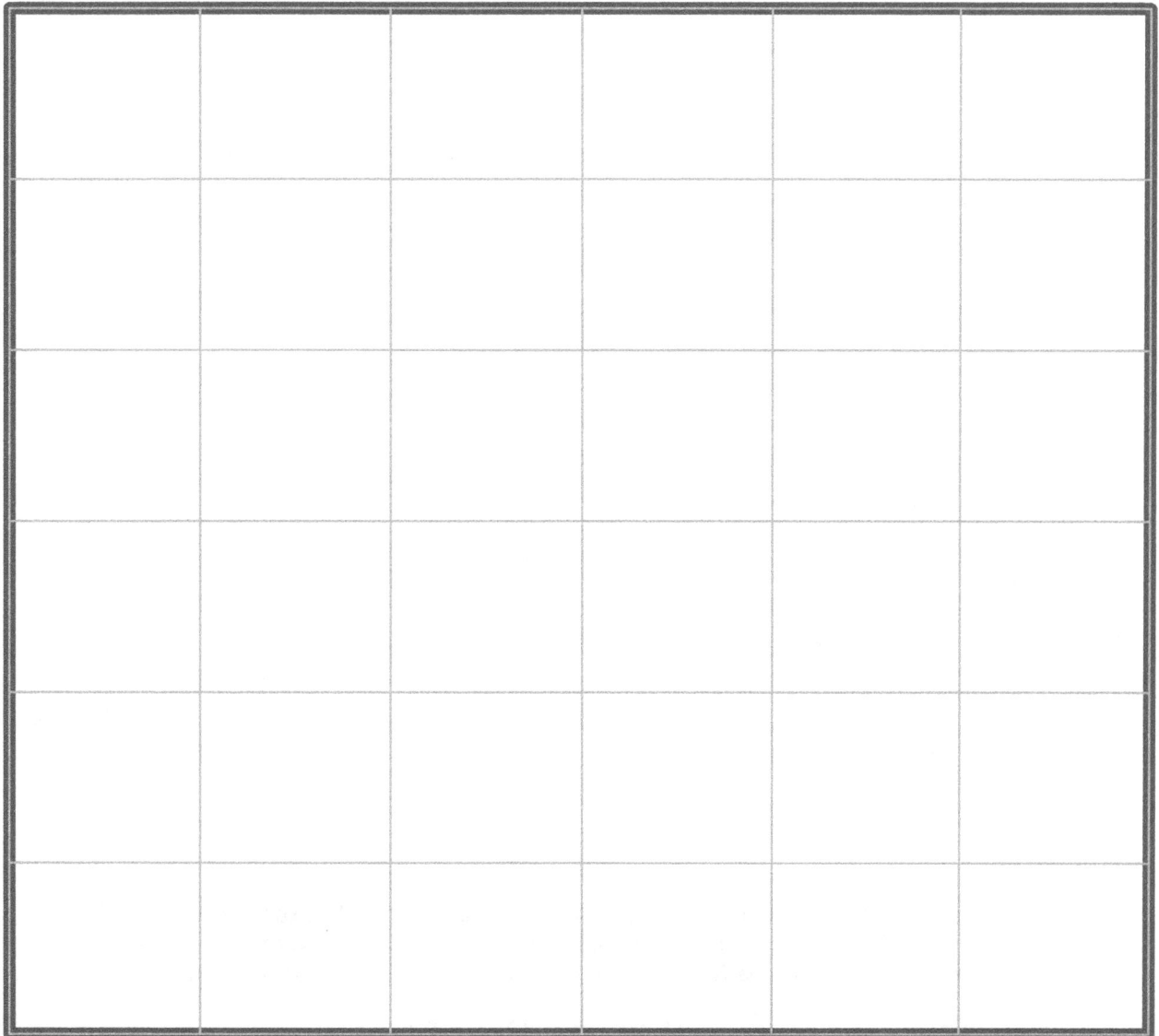

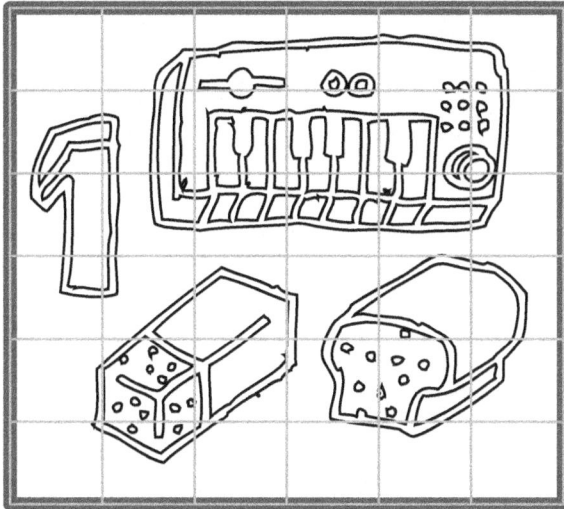

DRAW
THE
IMAGE

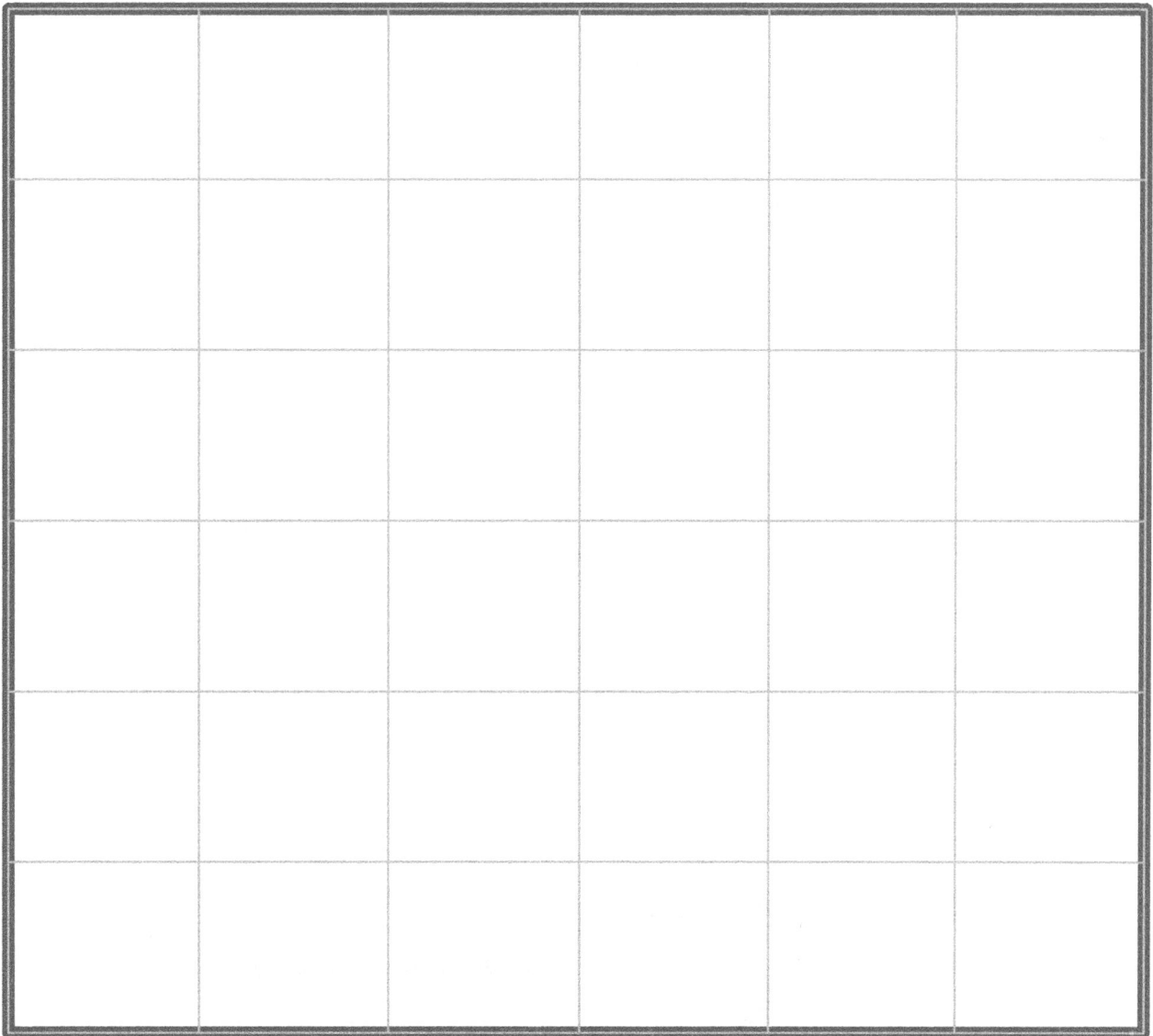

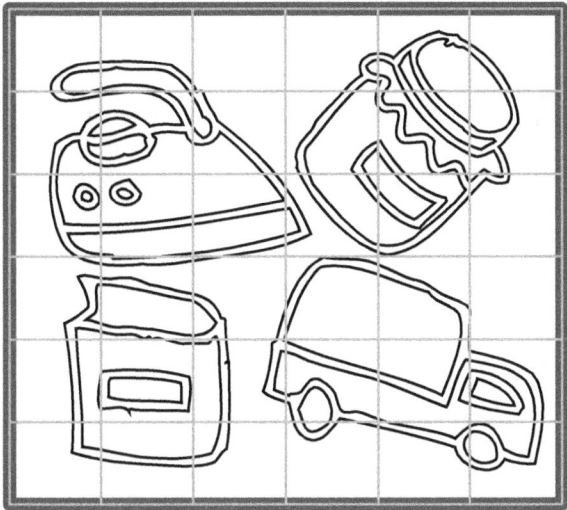

DRAW
THE
IMAGE

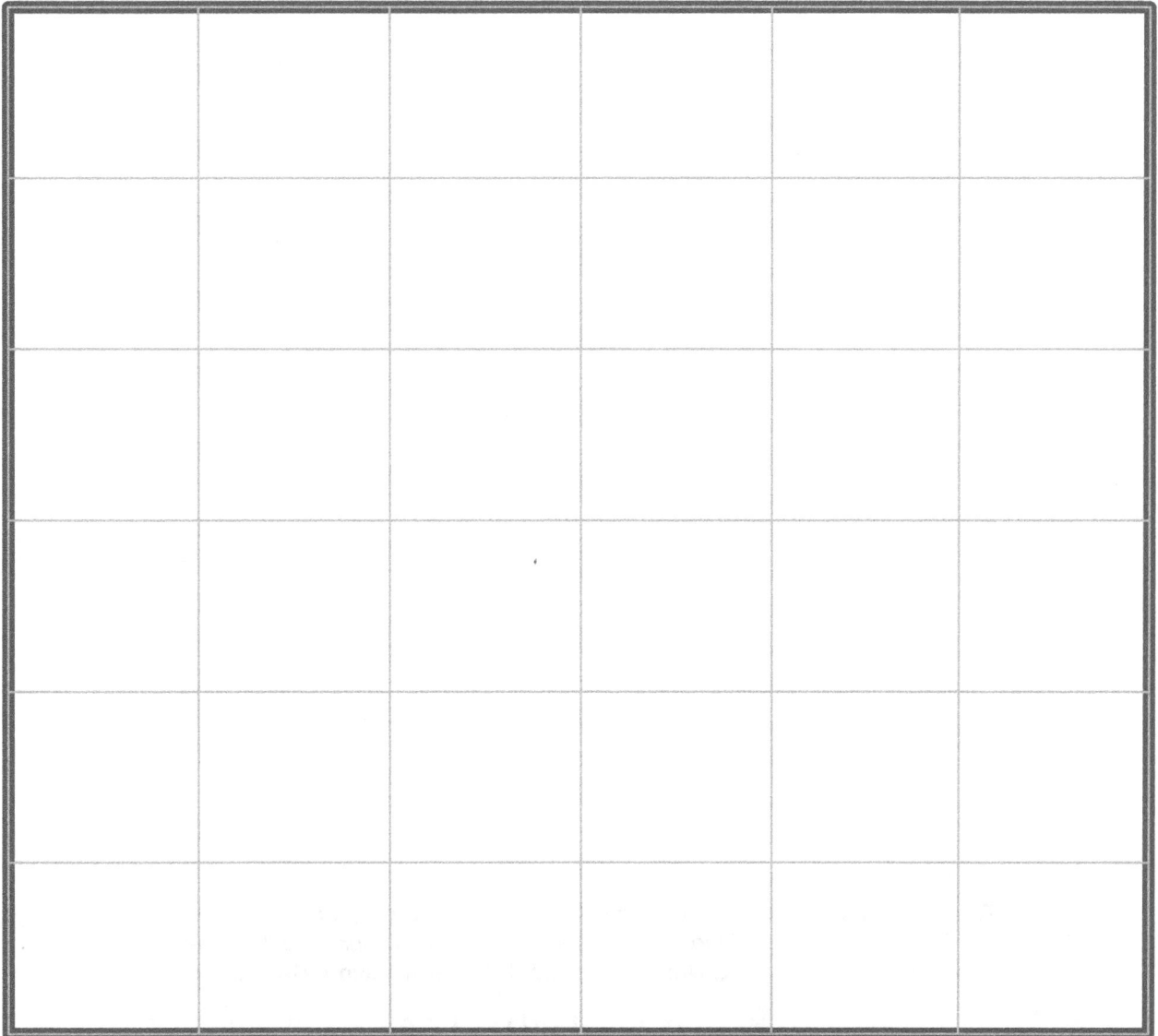

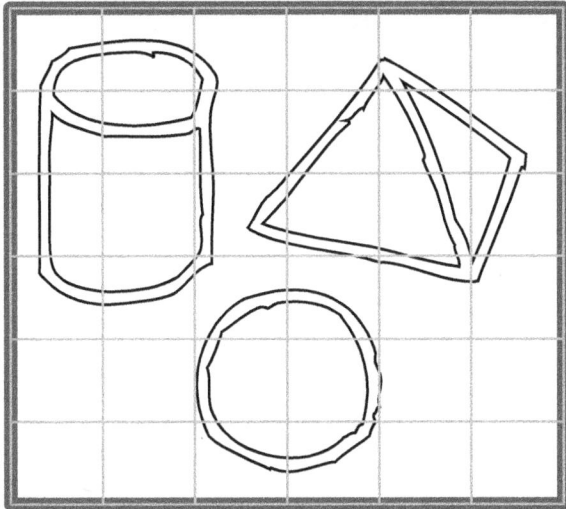

DRAW
THE
DOODLE
IMAGE

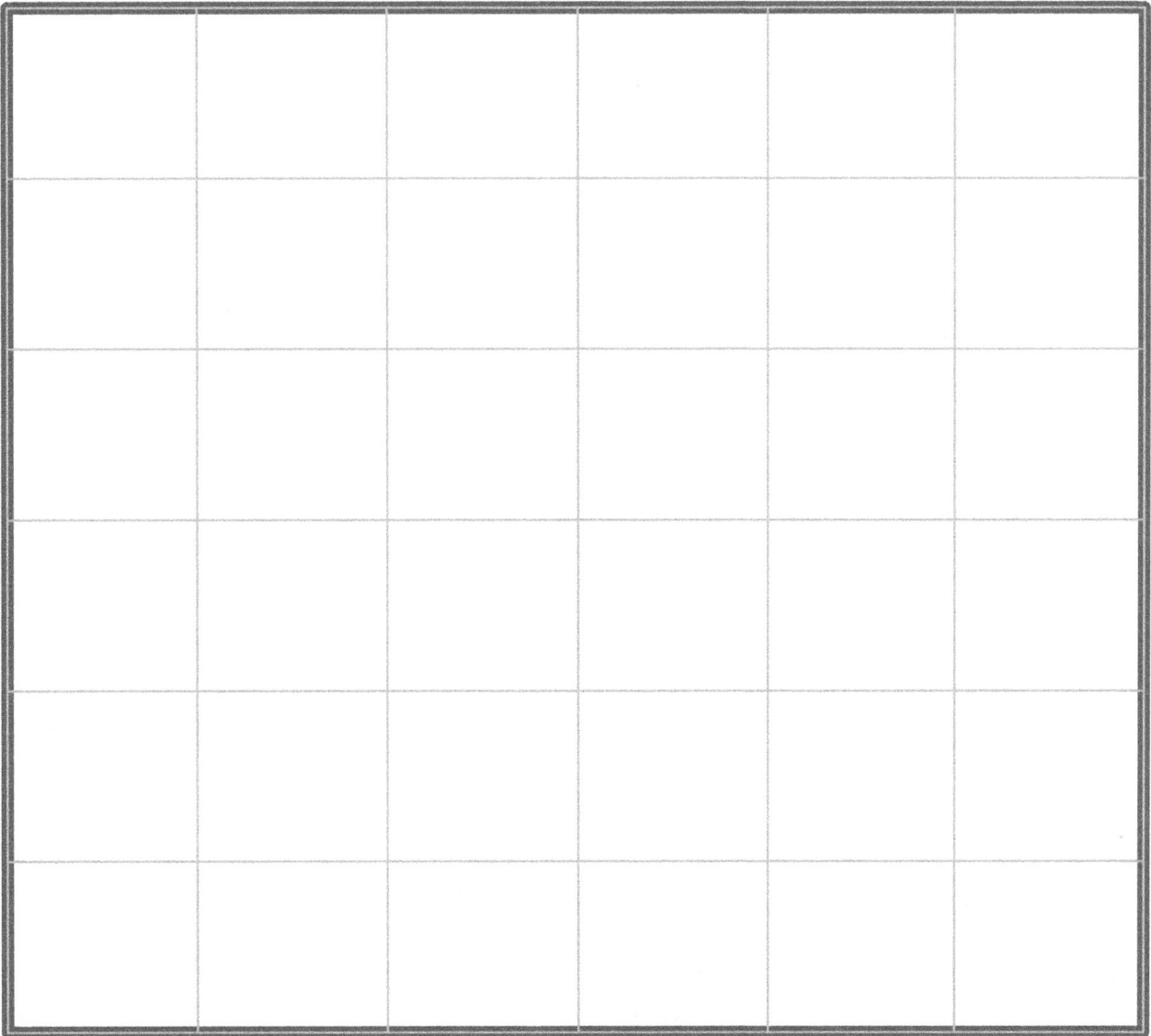

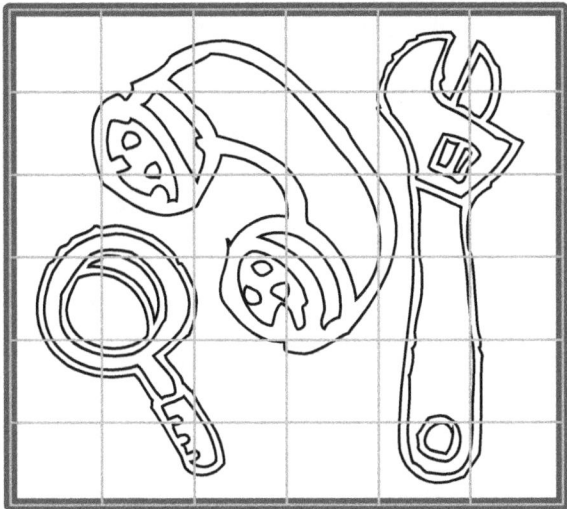

DRAW
THE
DOODLE
IMAGE

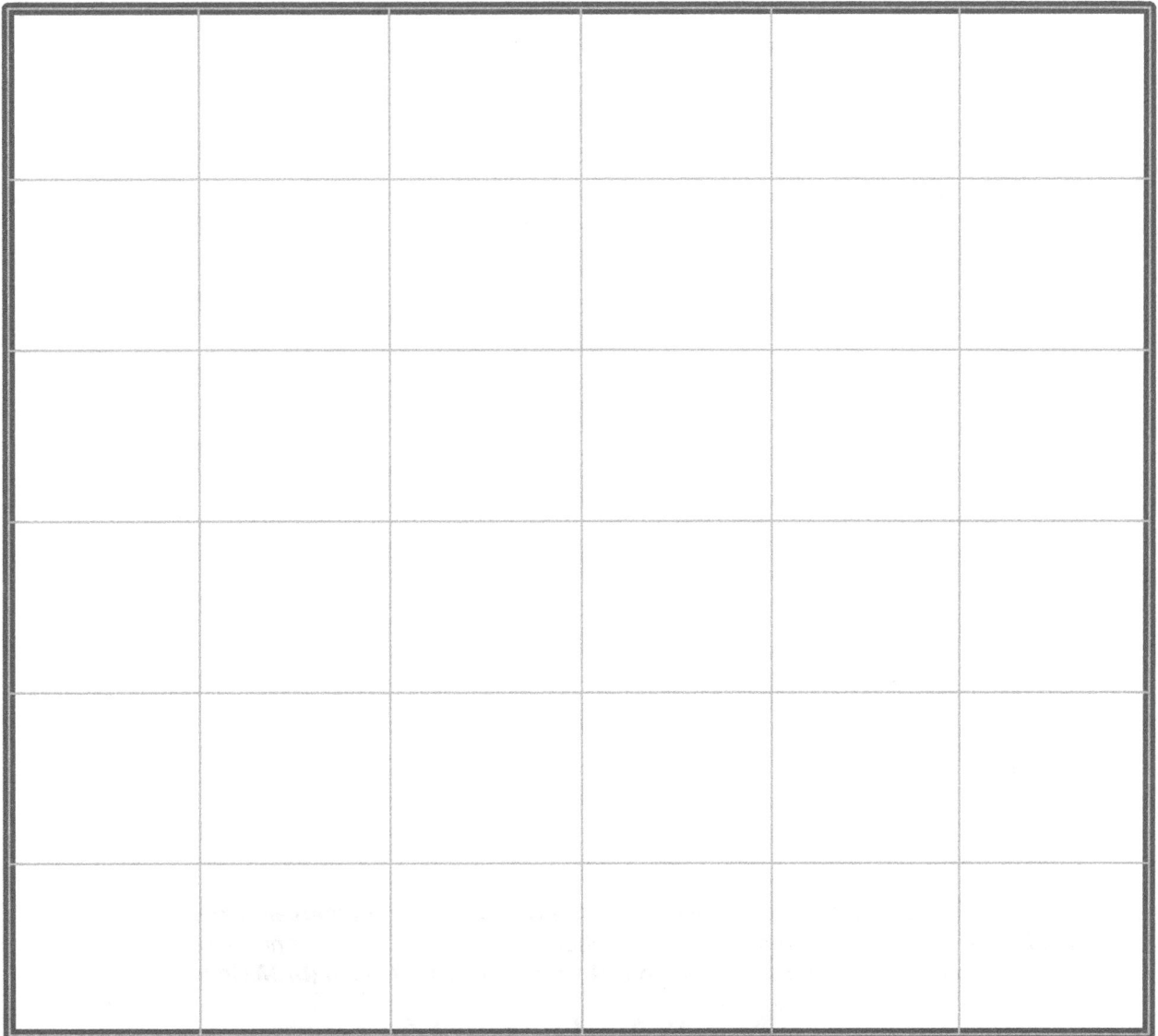

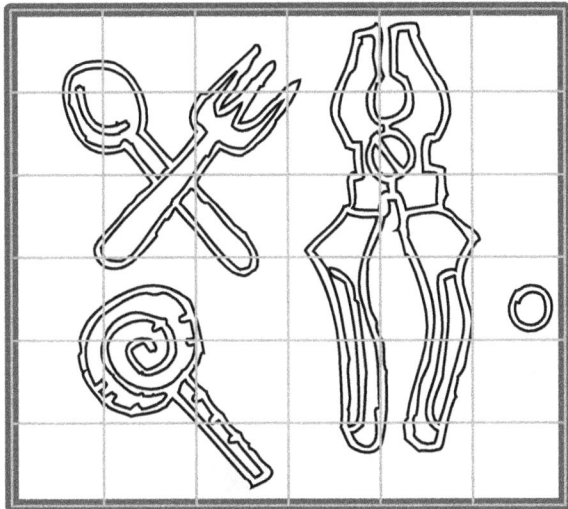

DRAW
THE
DOODLE
IMAGE

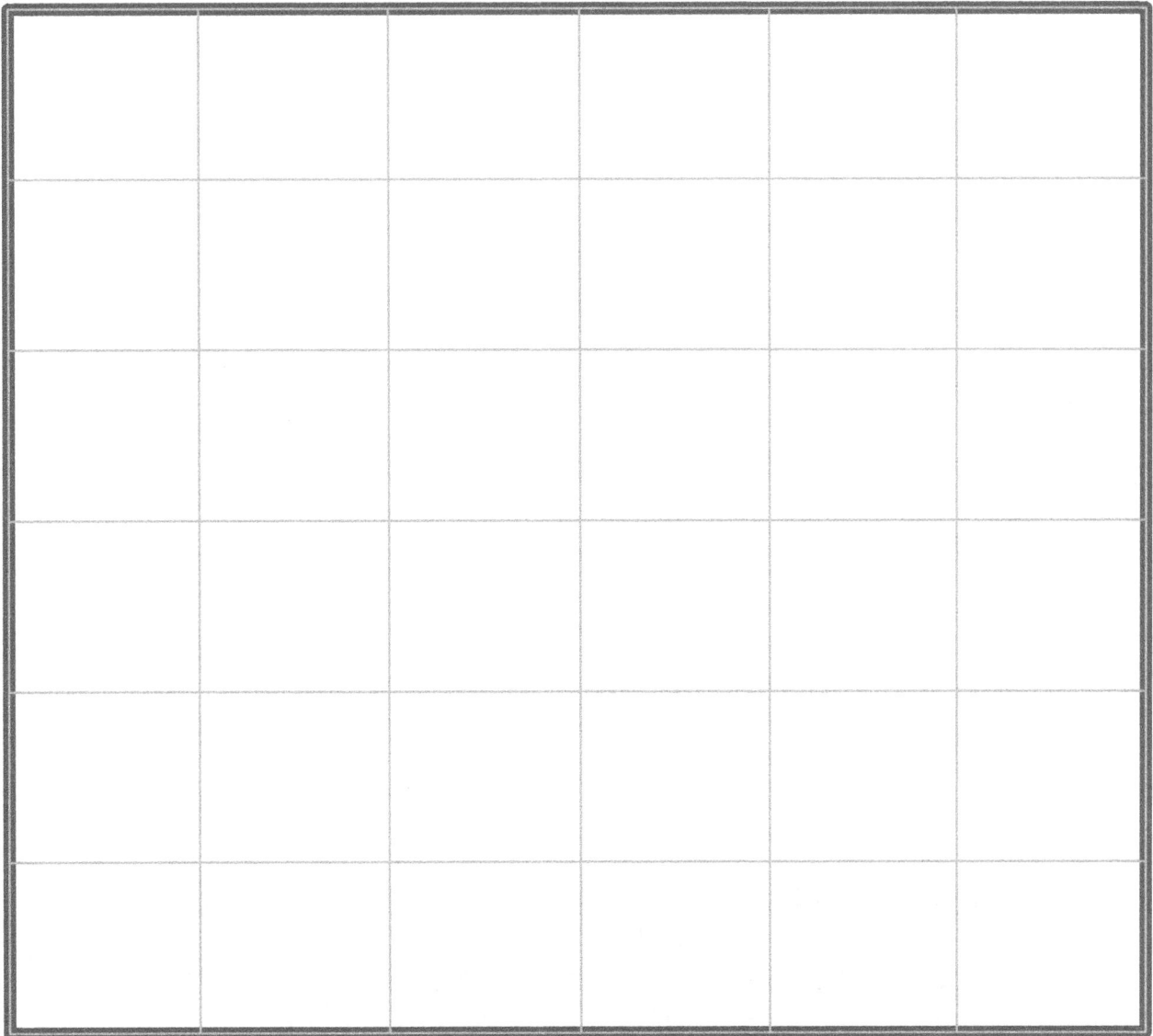

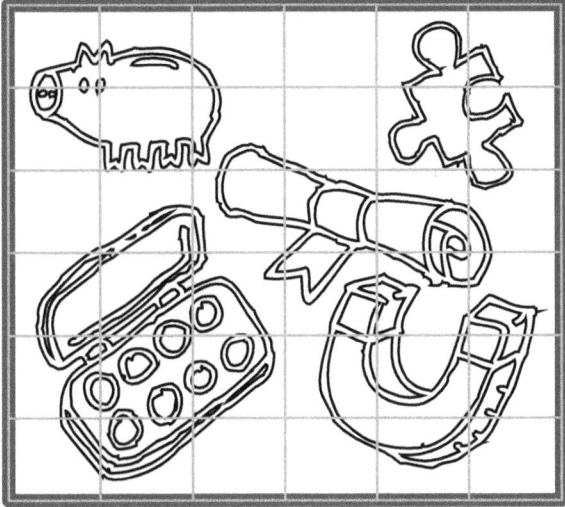

DRAW
THE
IMAGE

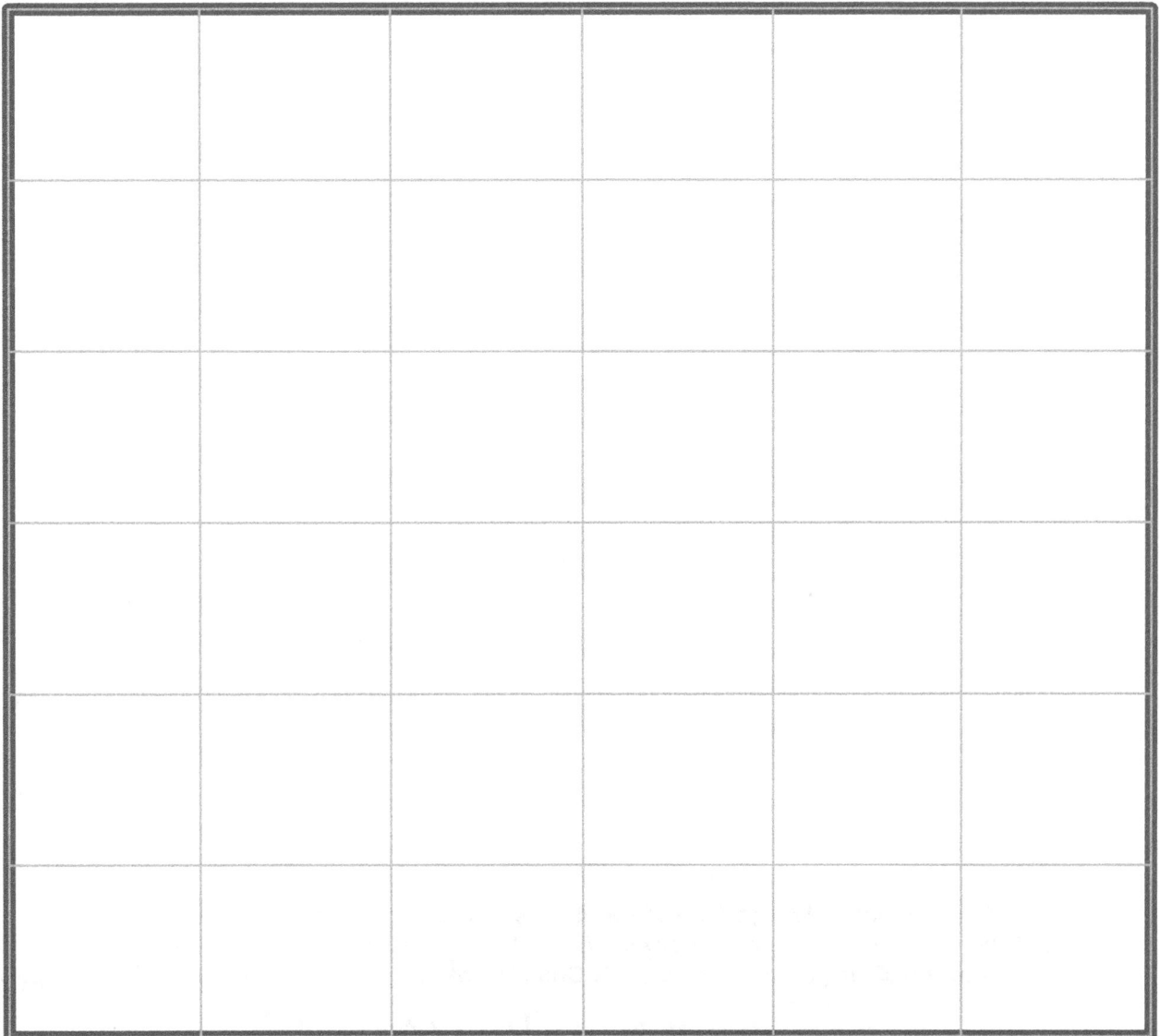

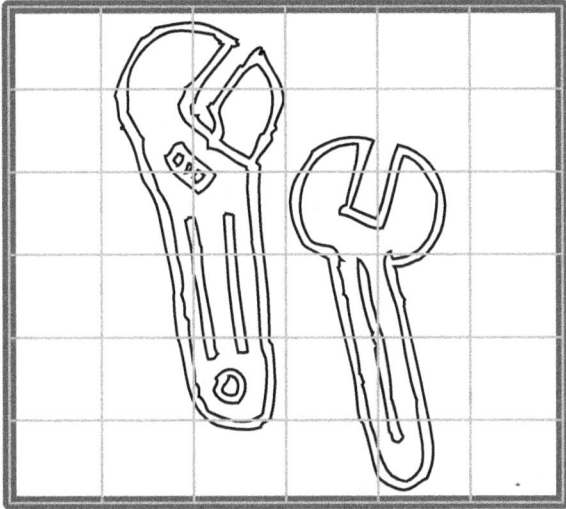

DRAW
THE
DOODLE
IMAGE

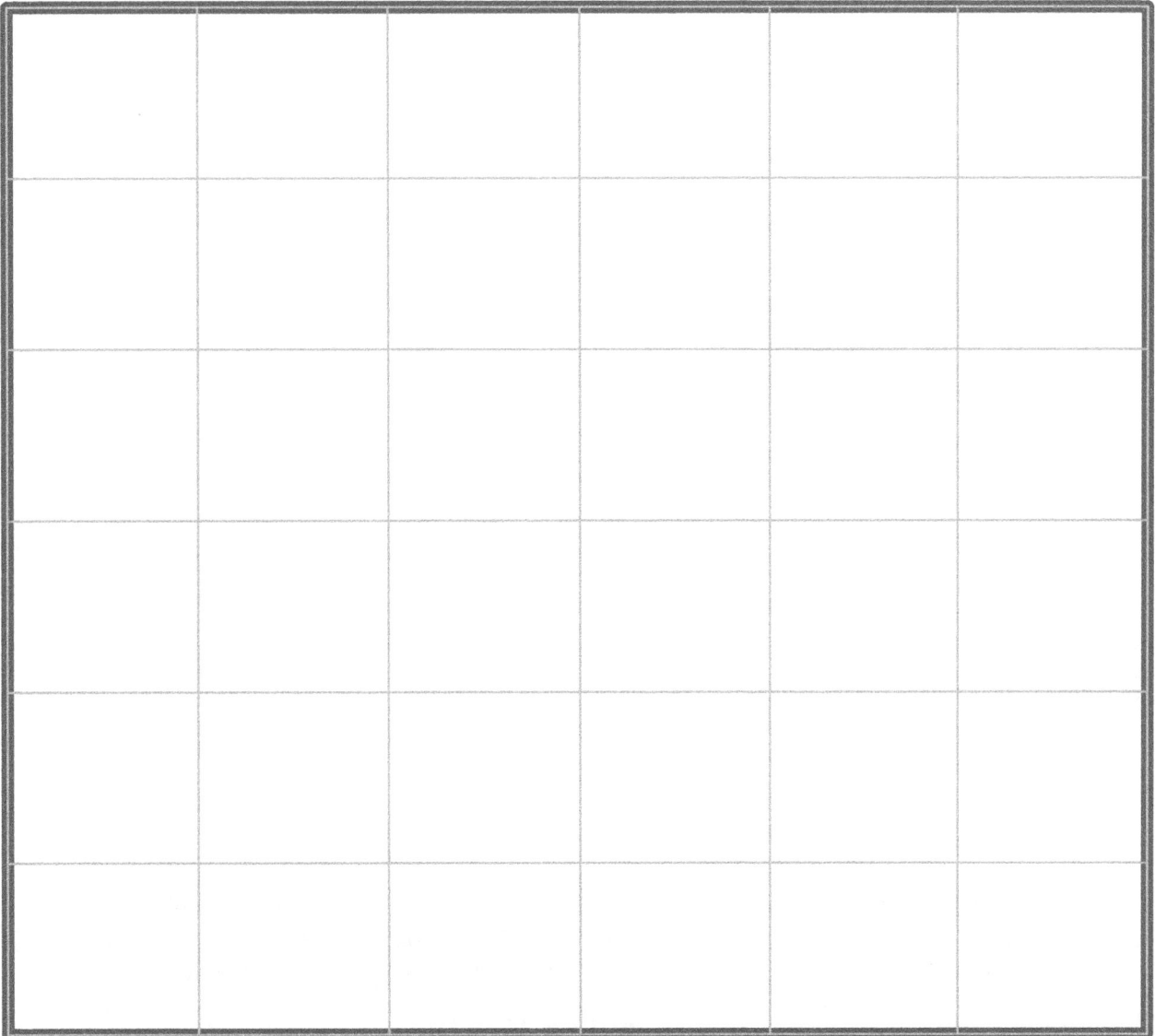

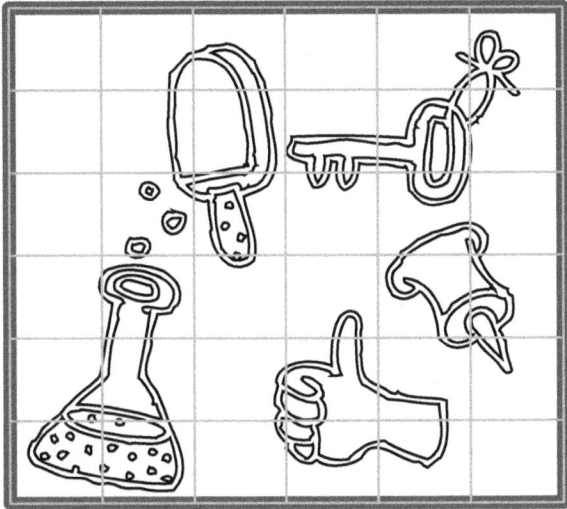

DRAW
THE
IMAGE

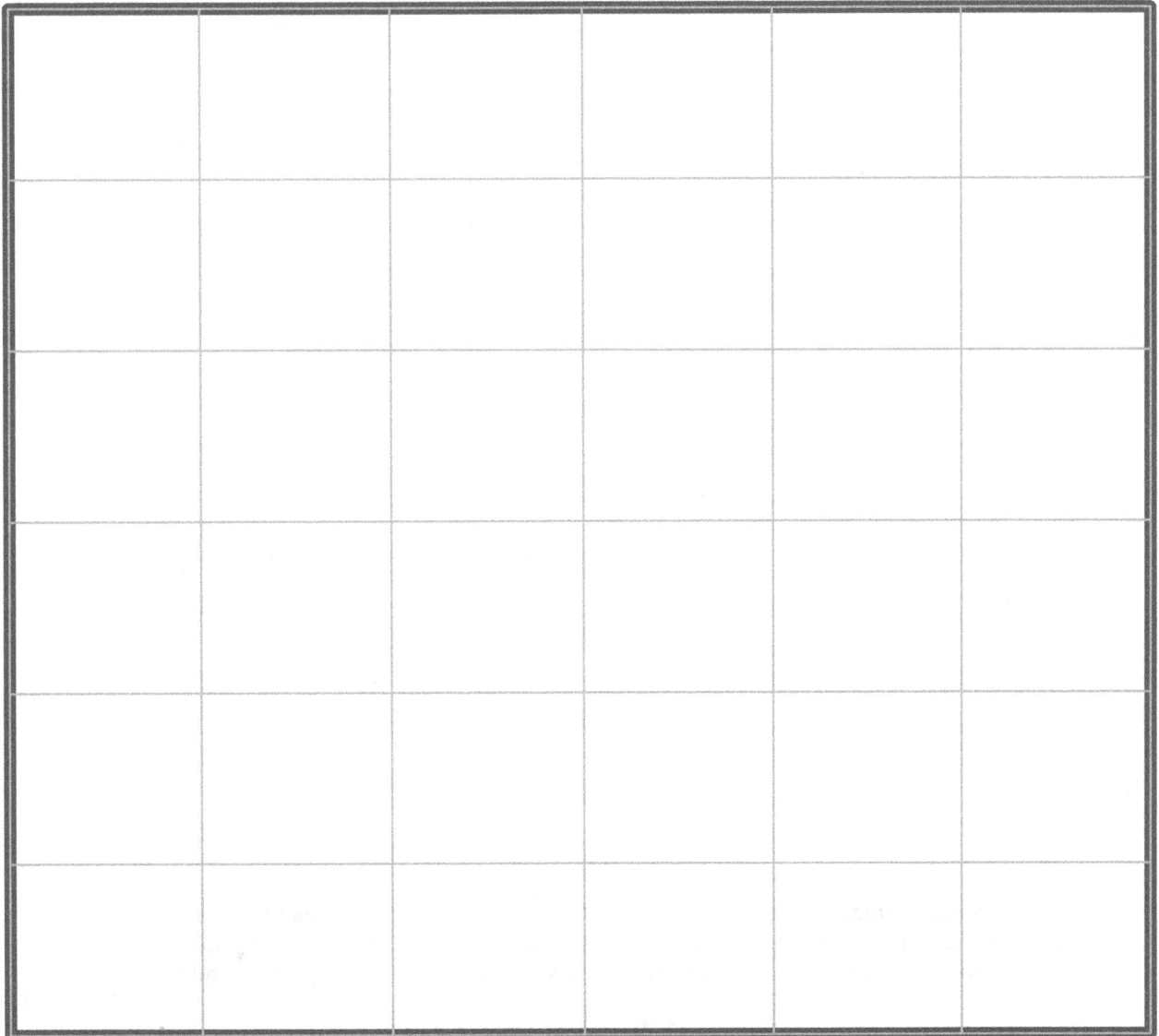

DRAW
THE
IMAGE

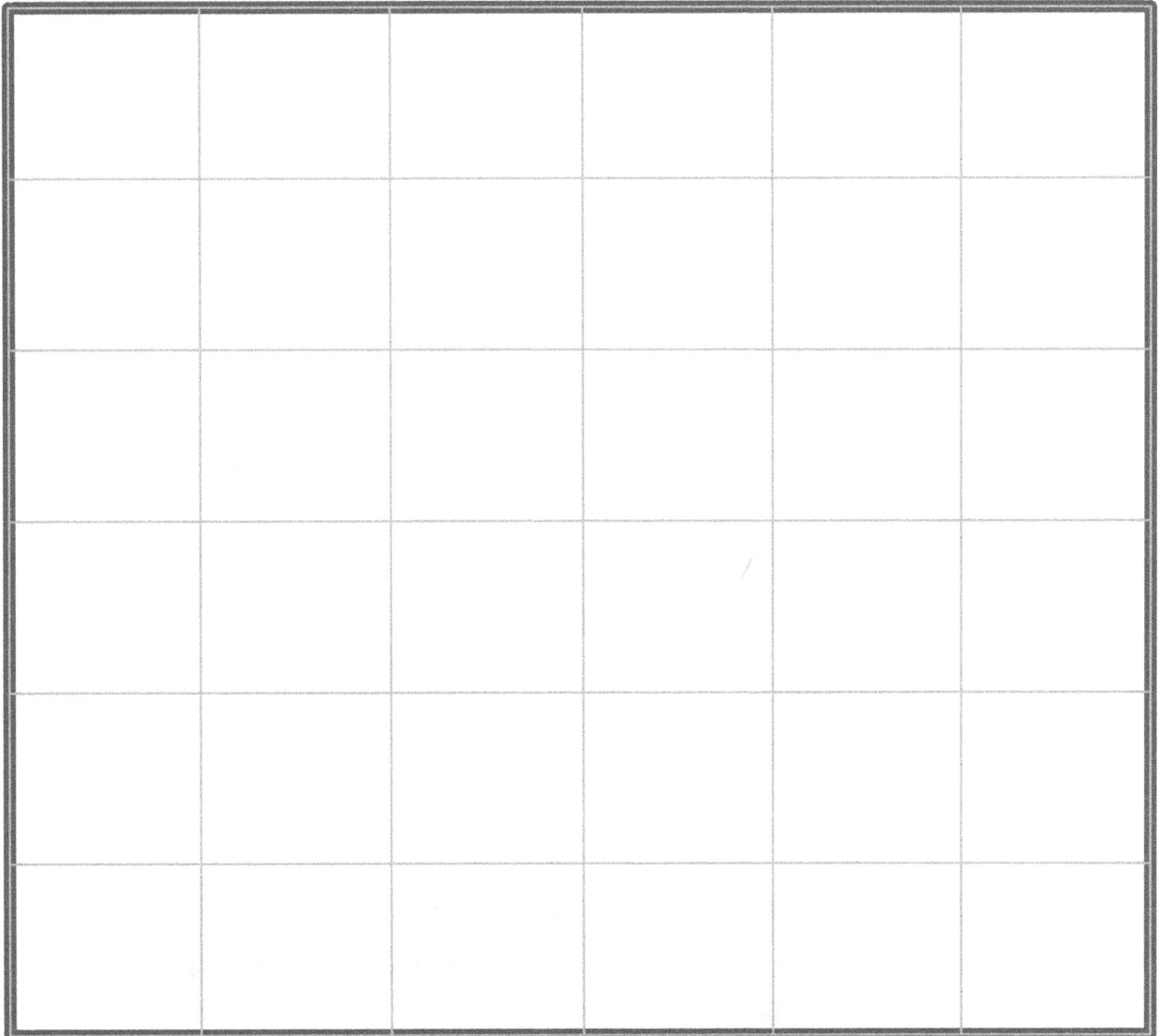

DRAW
THE
IMAGE

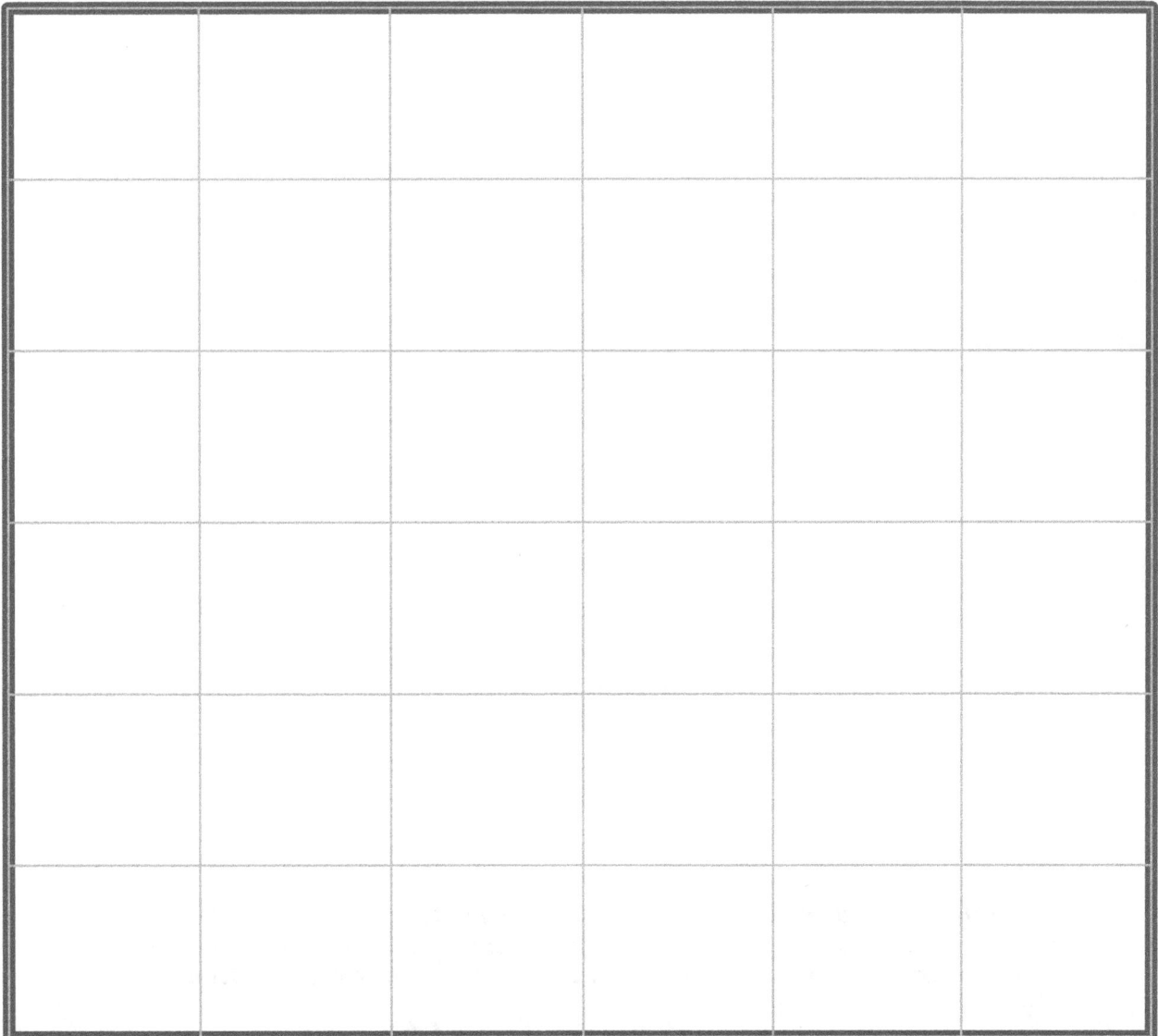

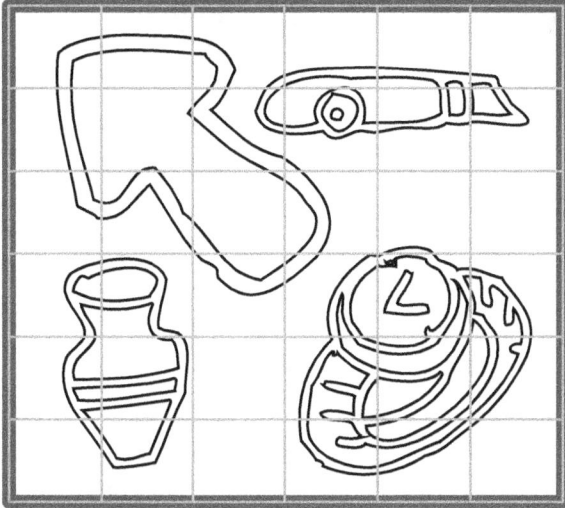

DRAW
THE
DOODLE
IMAGE

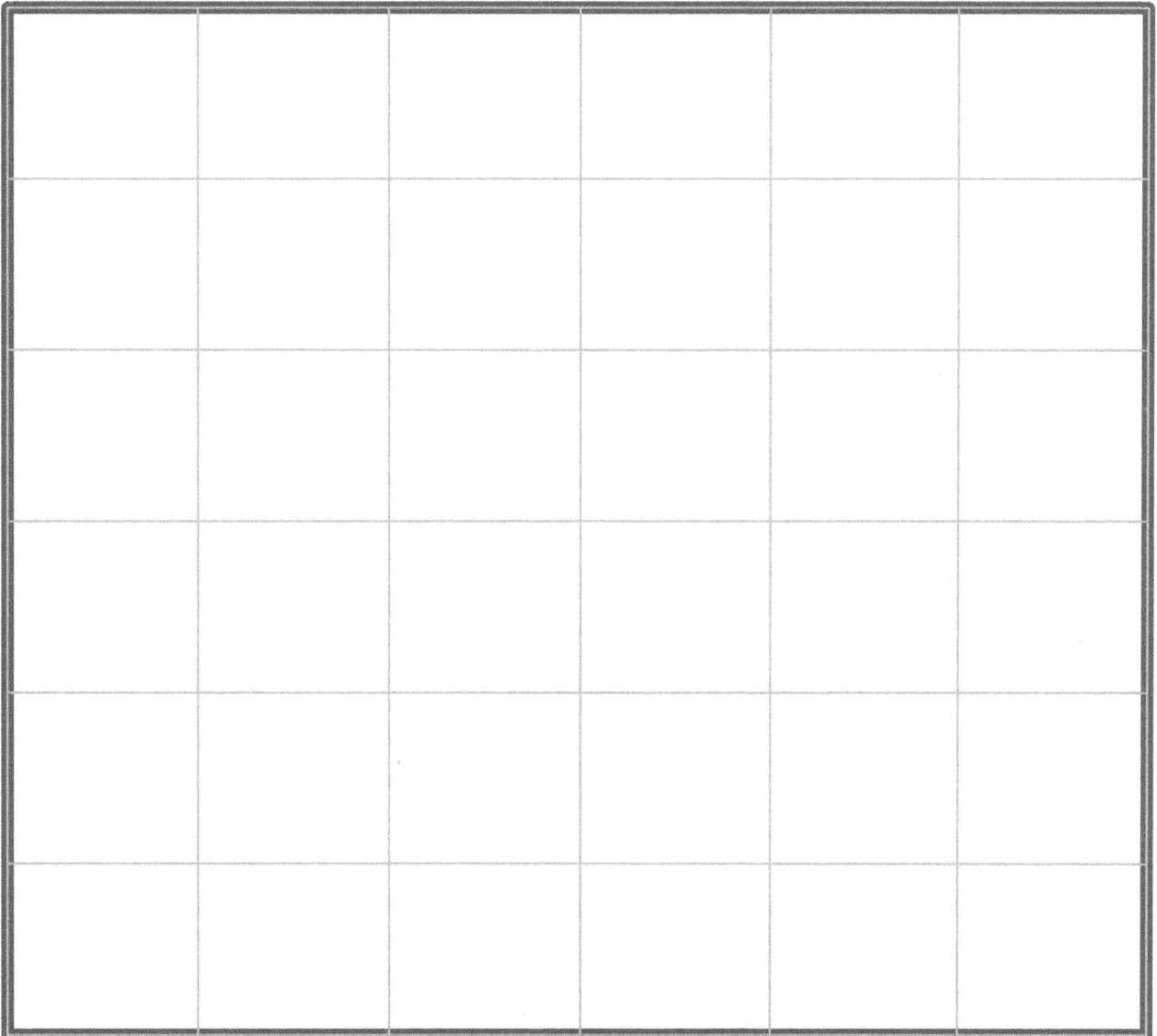

DRAW
THE
DOODLE
IMAGE

DRAW
THE
IMAGE

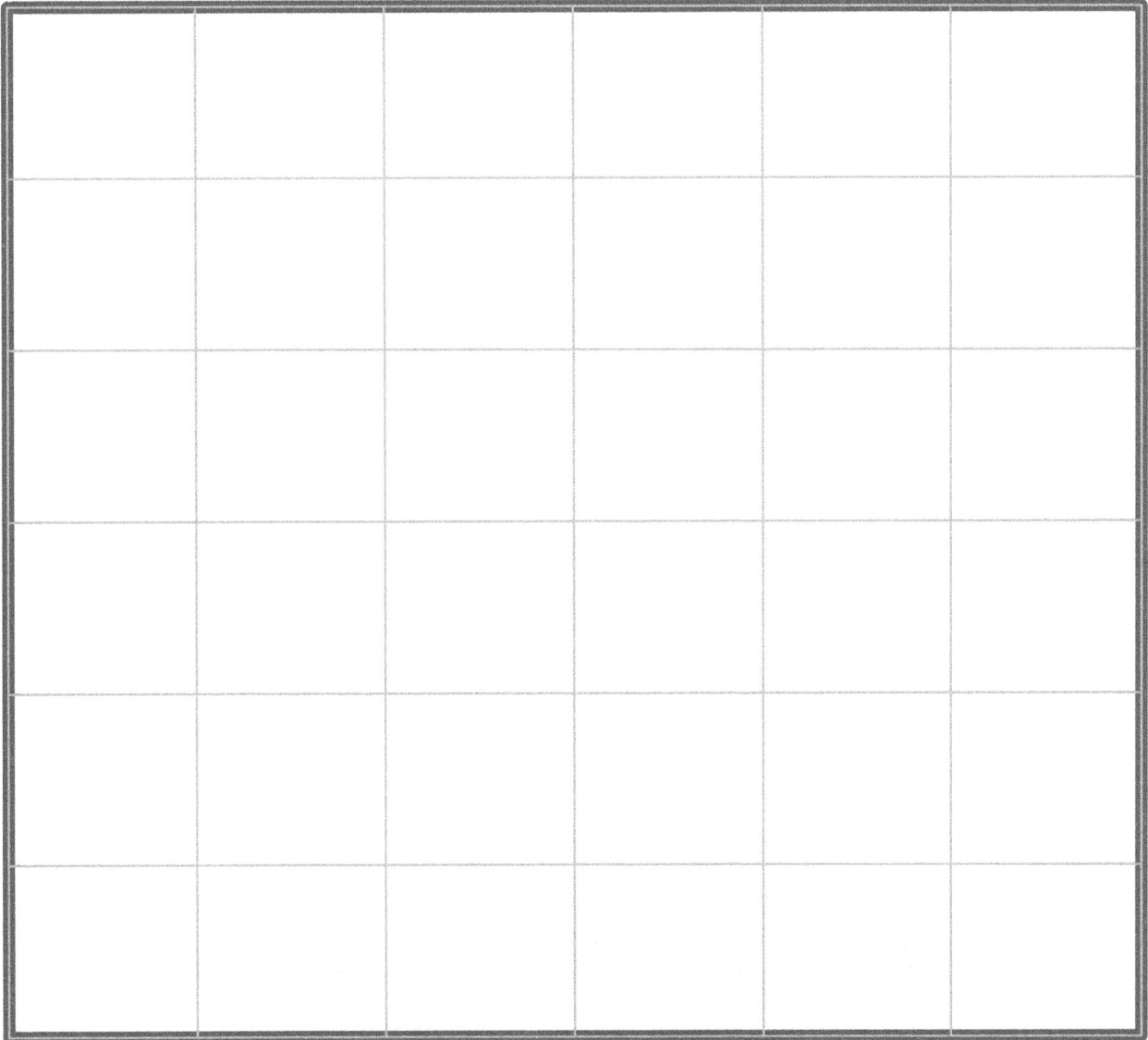

DRAW
THE
DOODLE
IMAGE

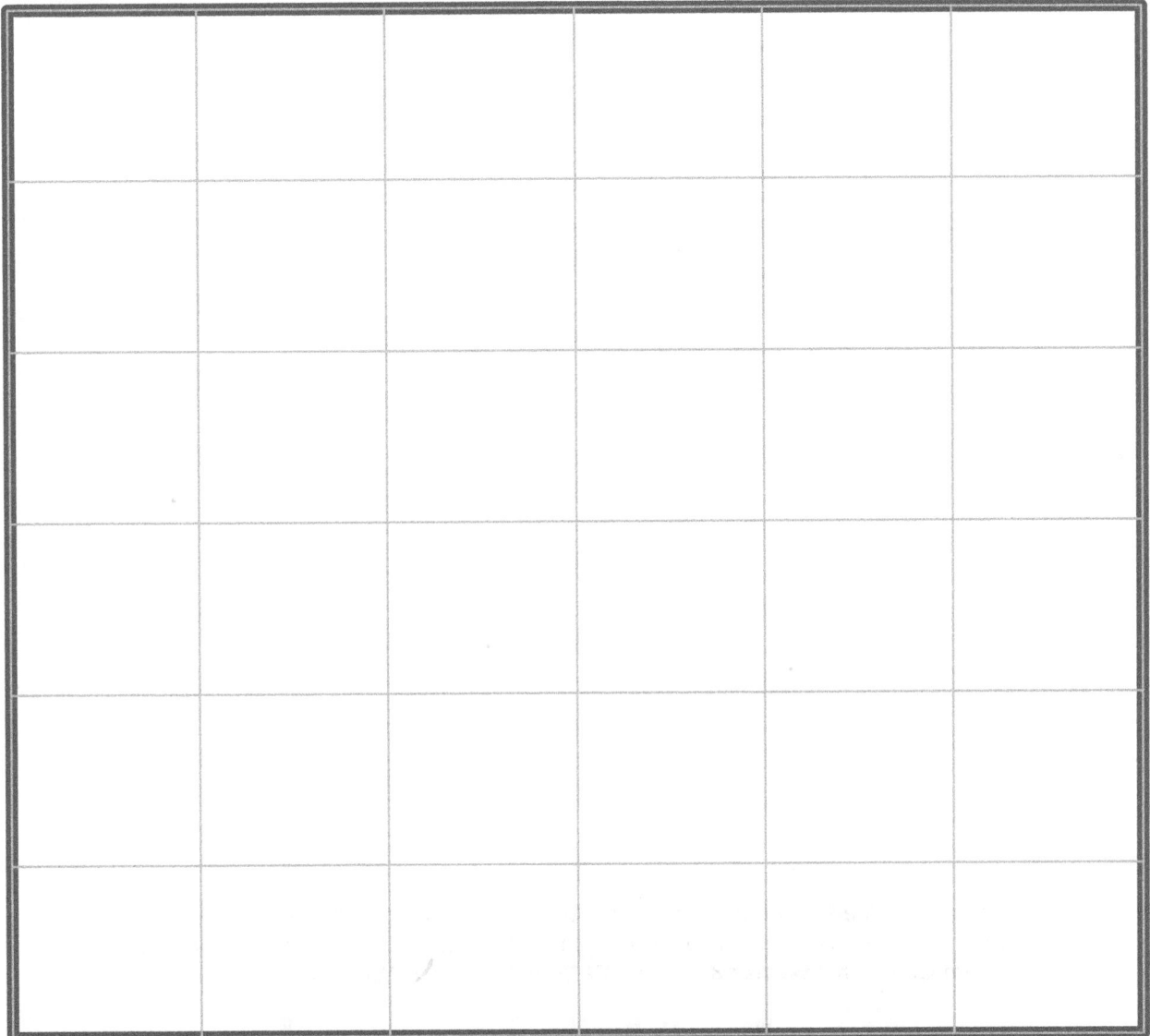

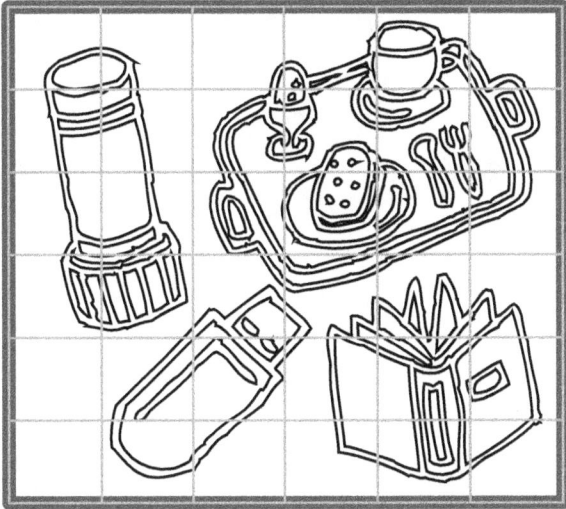

DRAW
THE
IMAGE

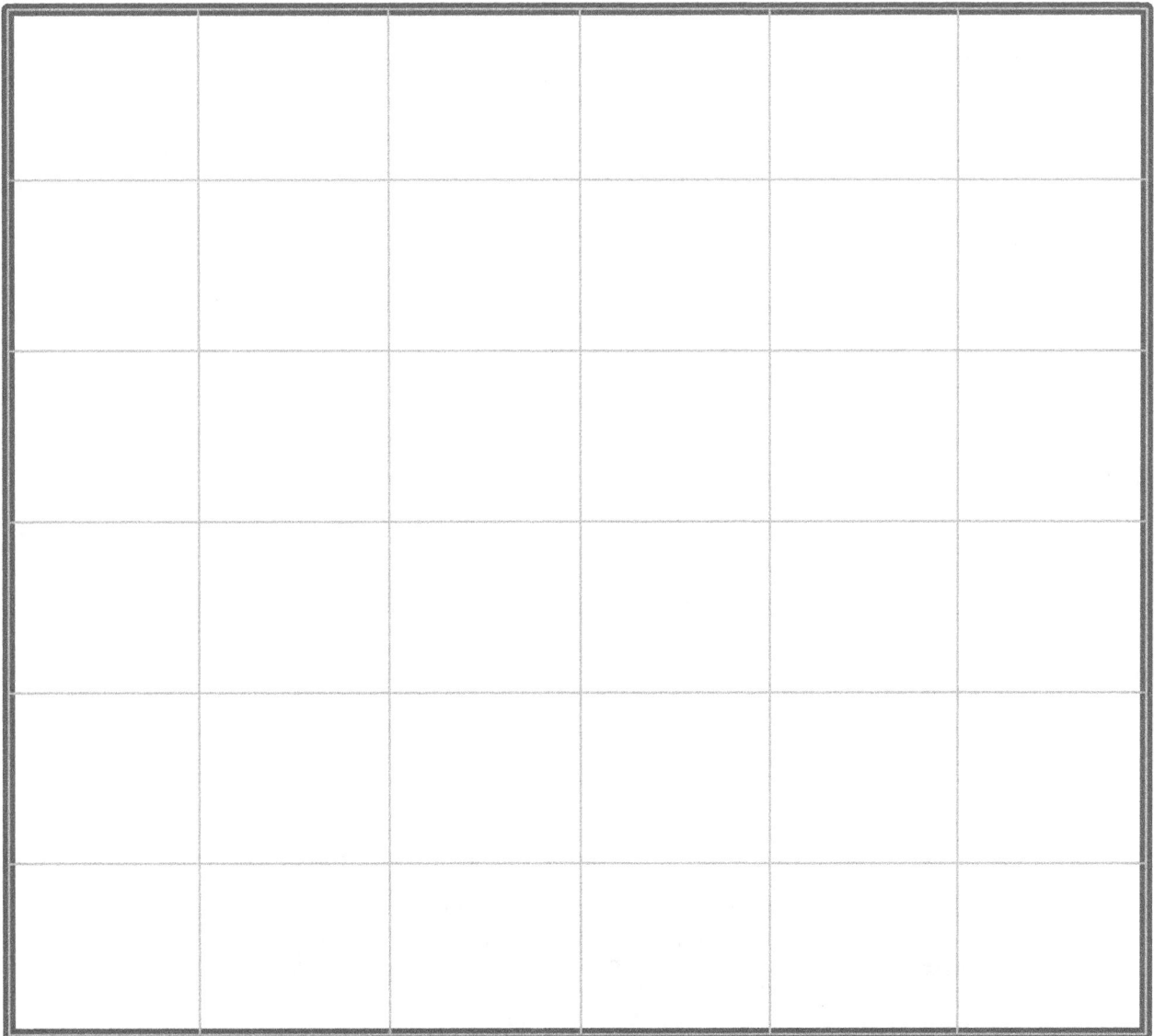

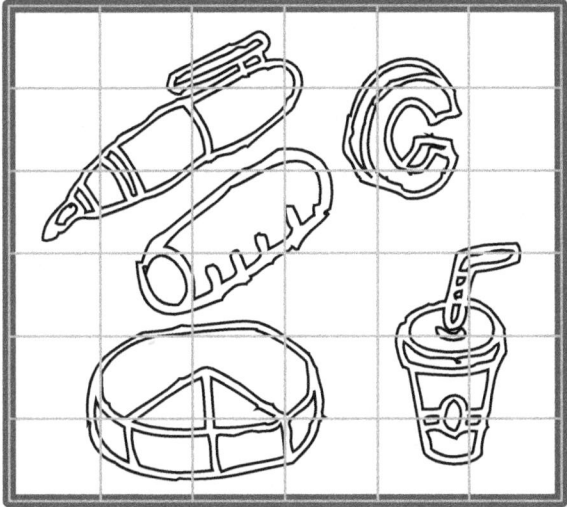

DRAW
THE
IMAGE

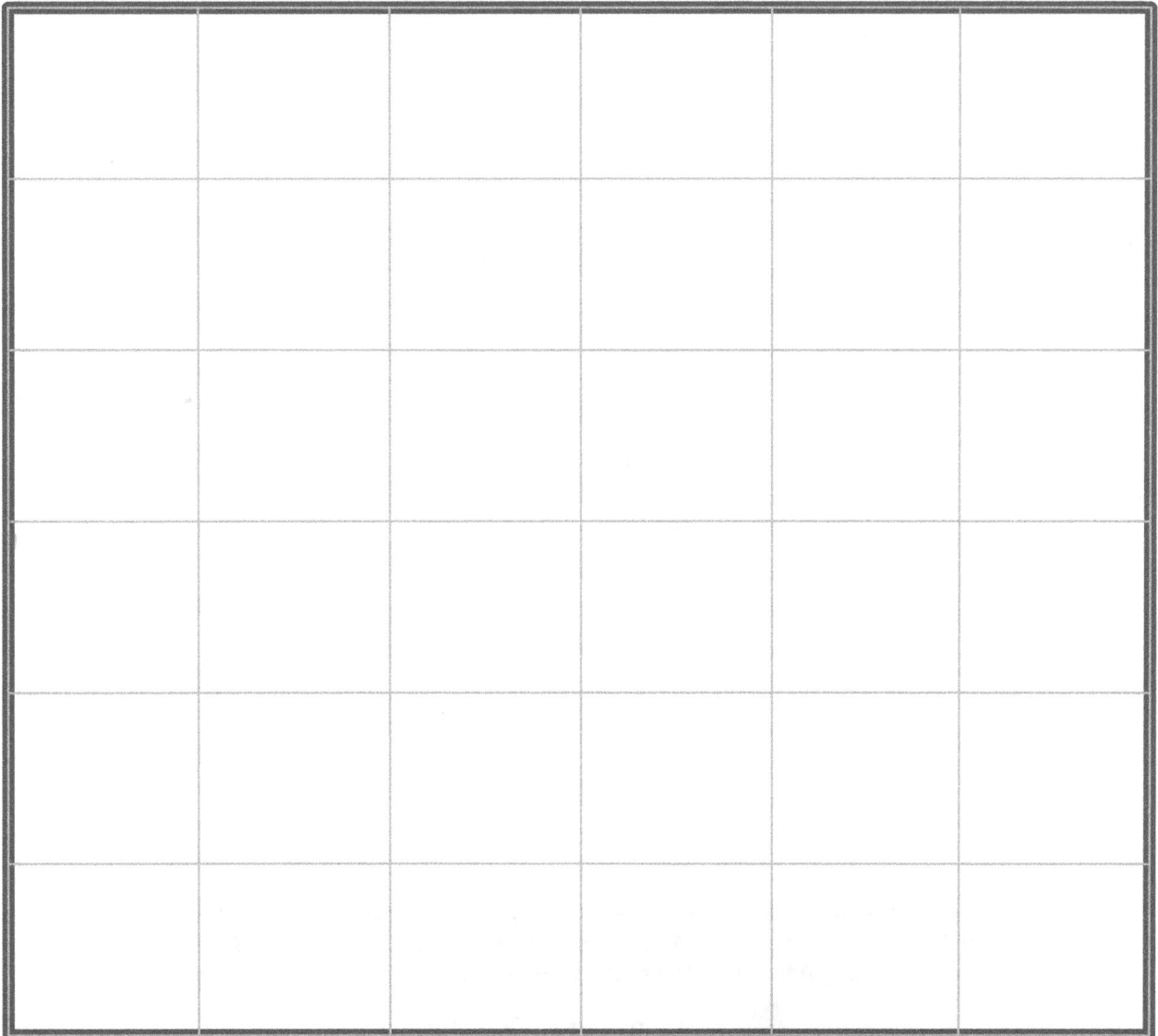

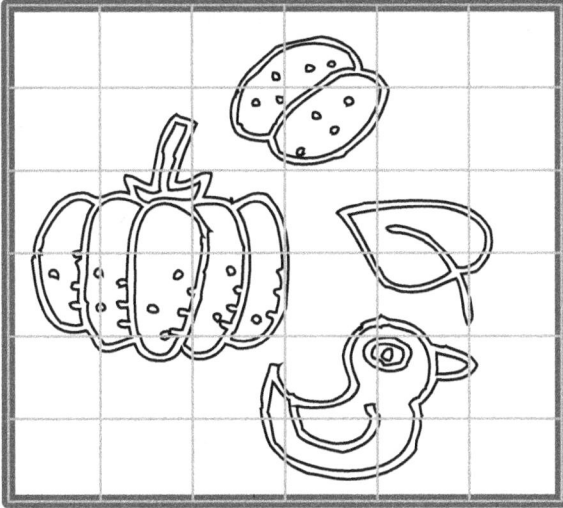

DRAW
THE
DOODLE
IMAGE

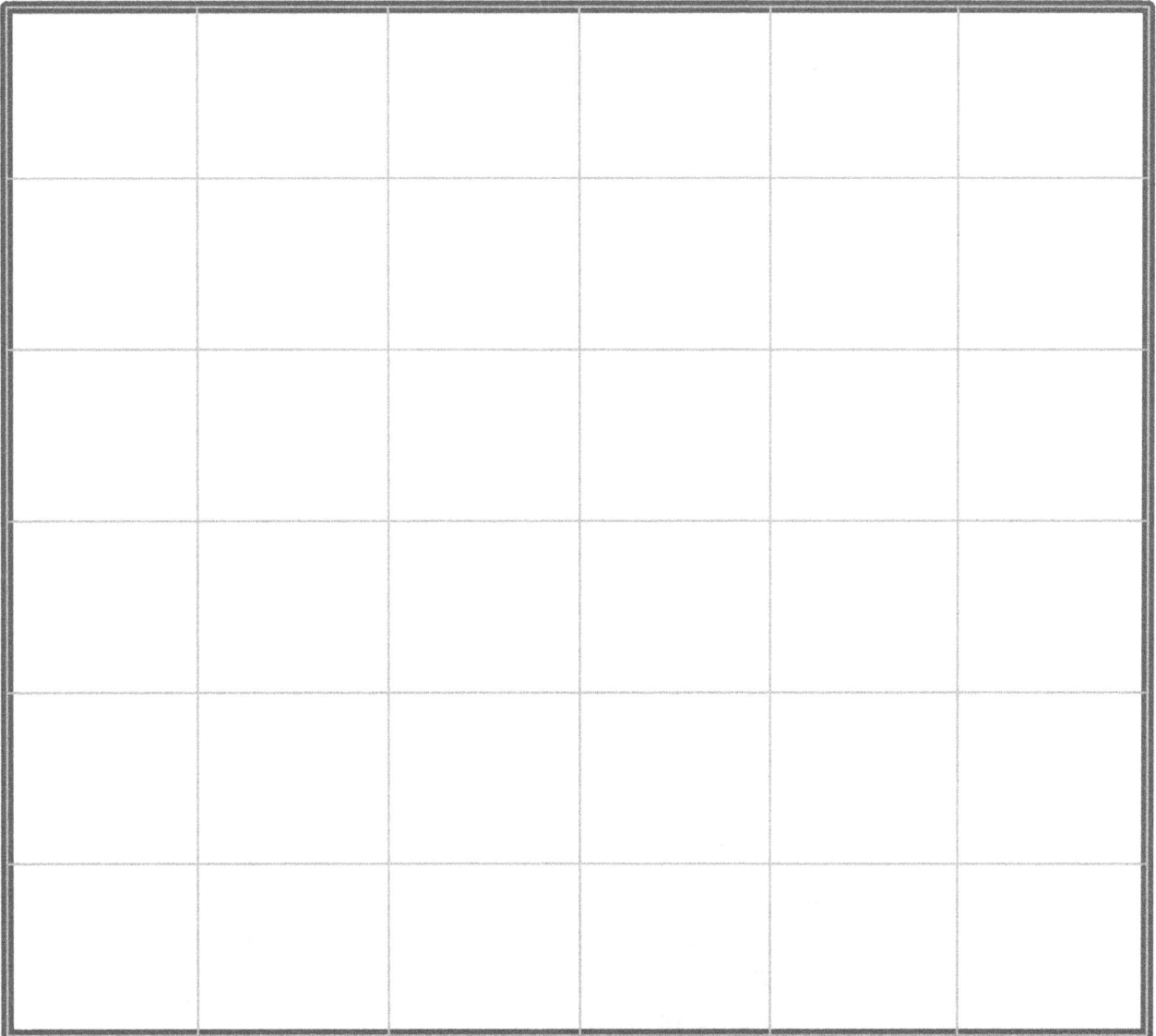

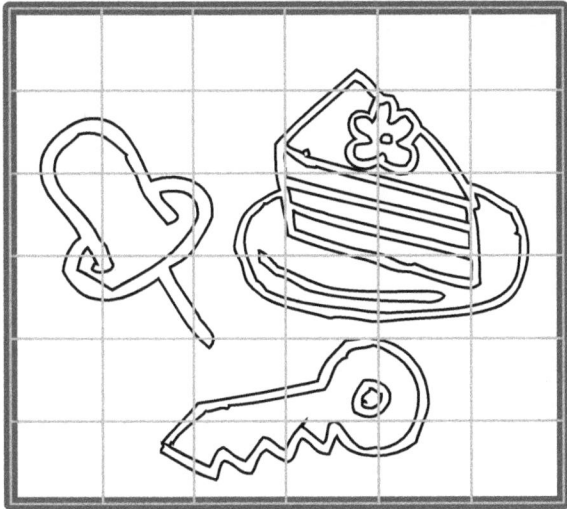

DRAW
THE
DOODLE
IMAGE

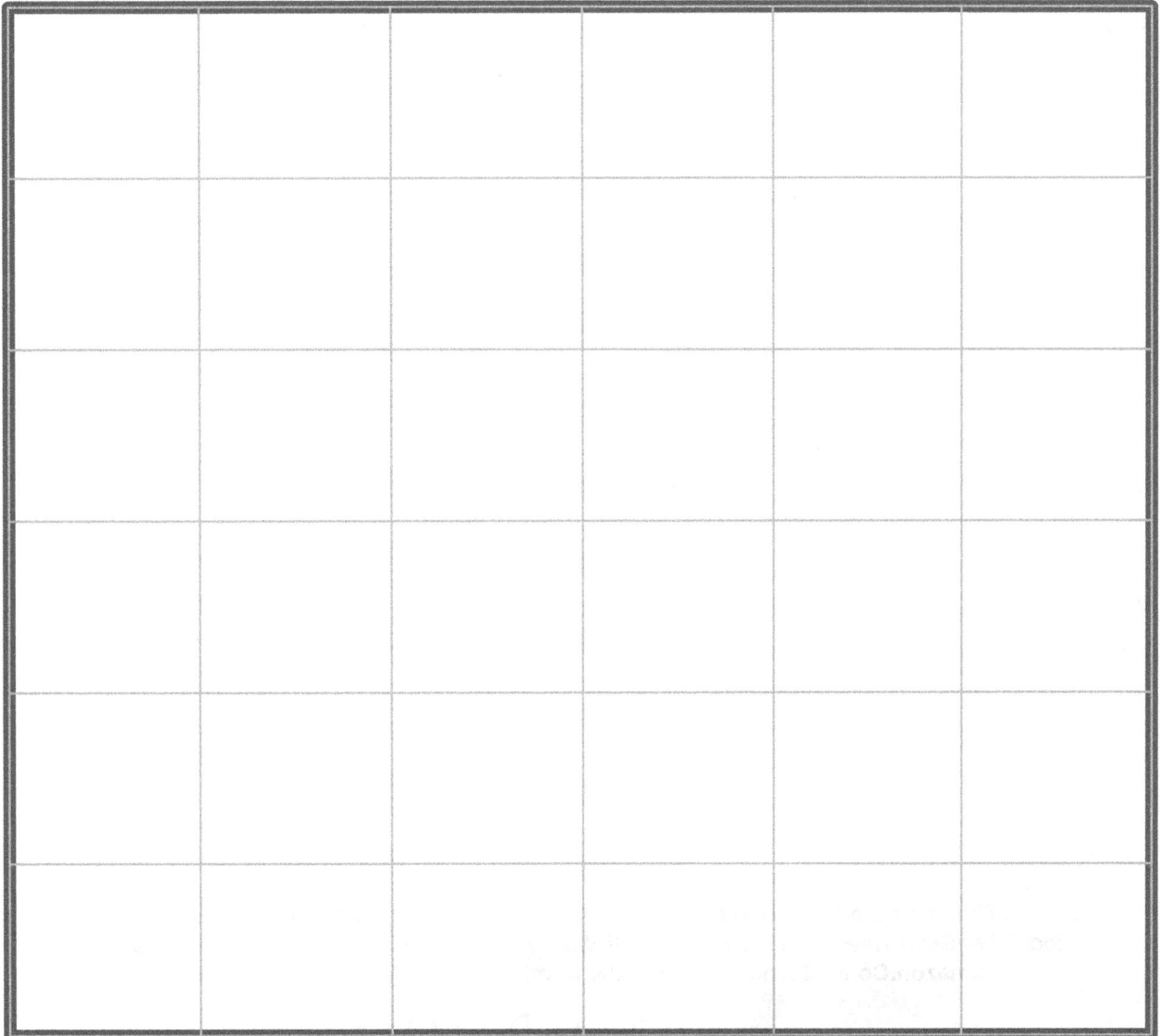

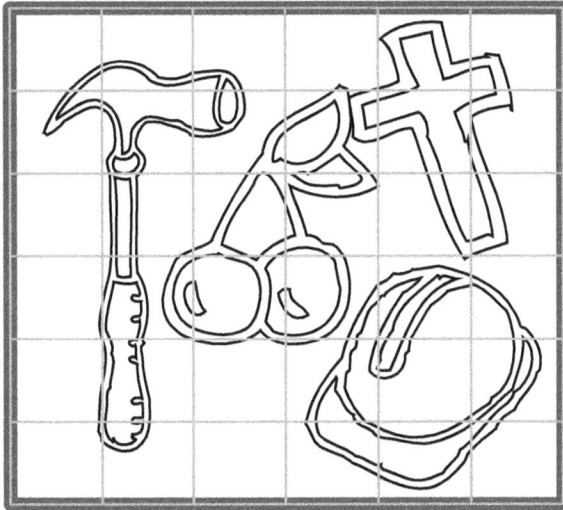

DRAW
THE
DOODLE
IMAGE

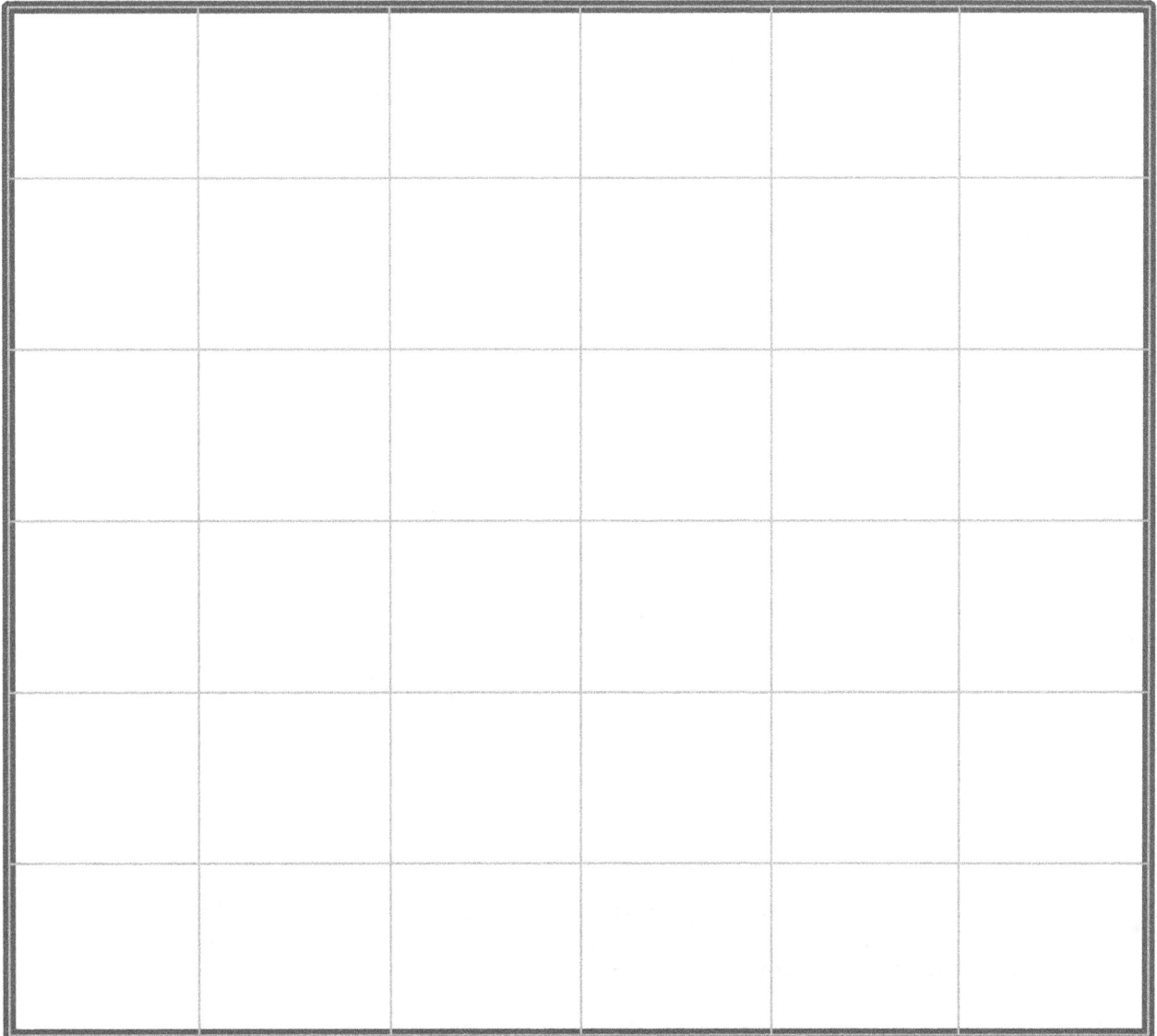

DRAW
THE
IMAGE

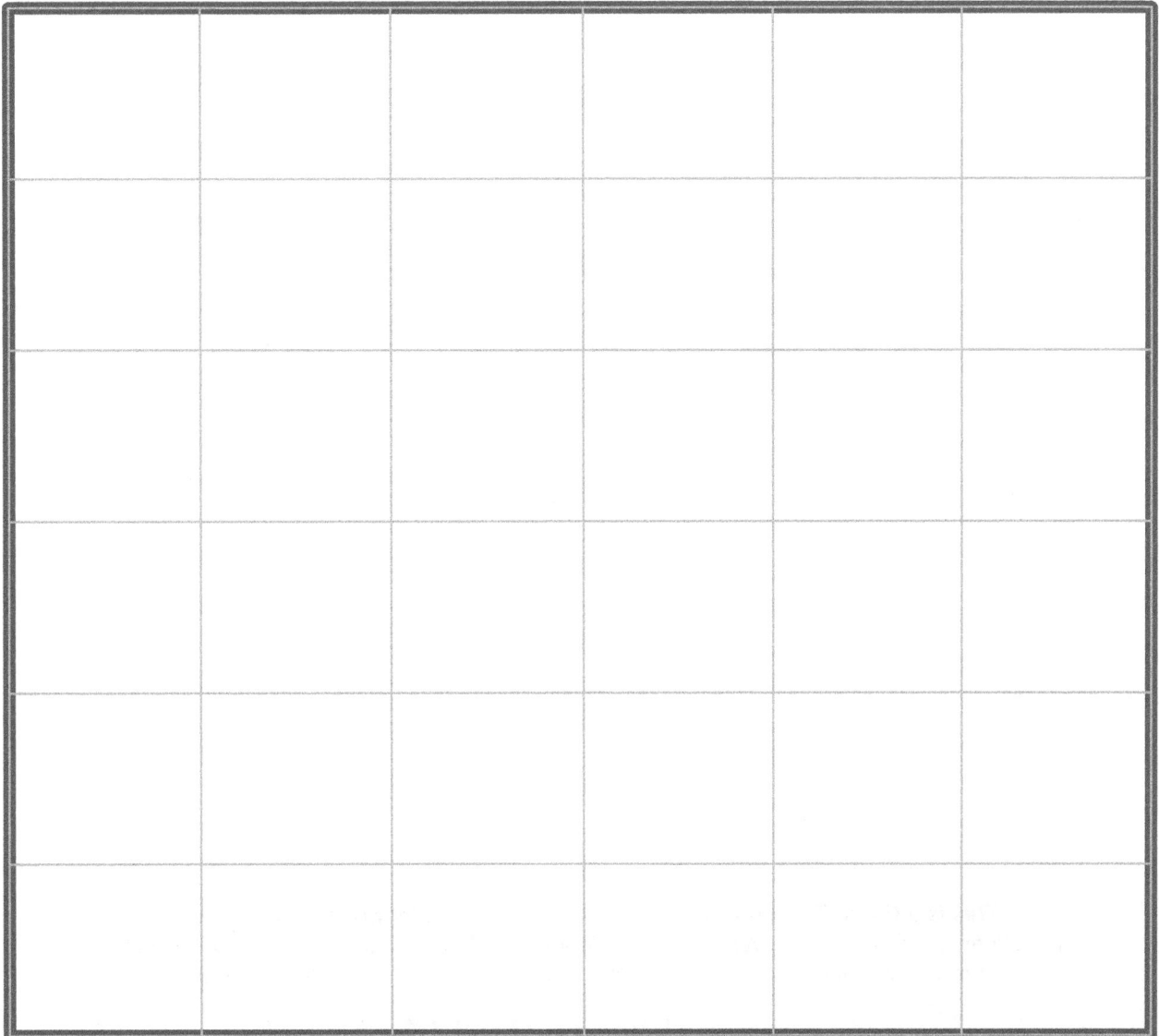

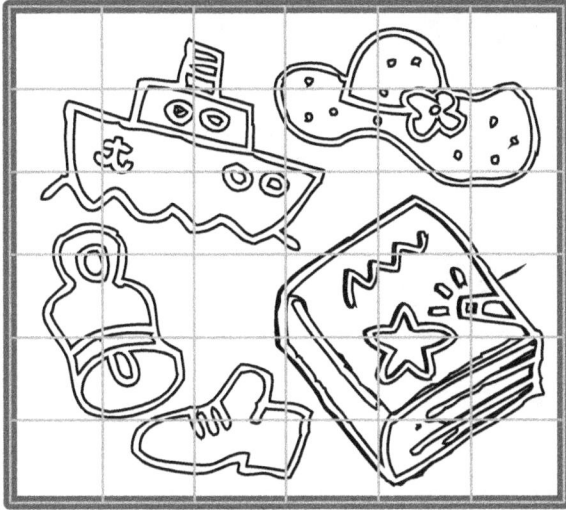

DRAW
THE
IMAGE

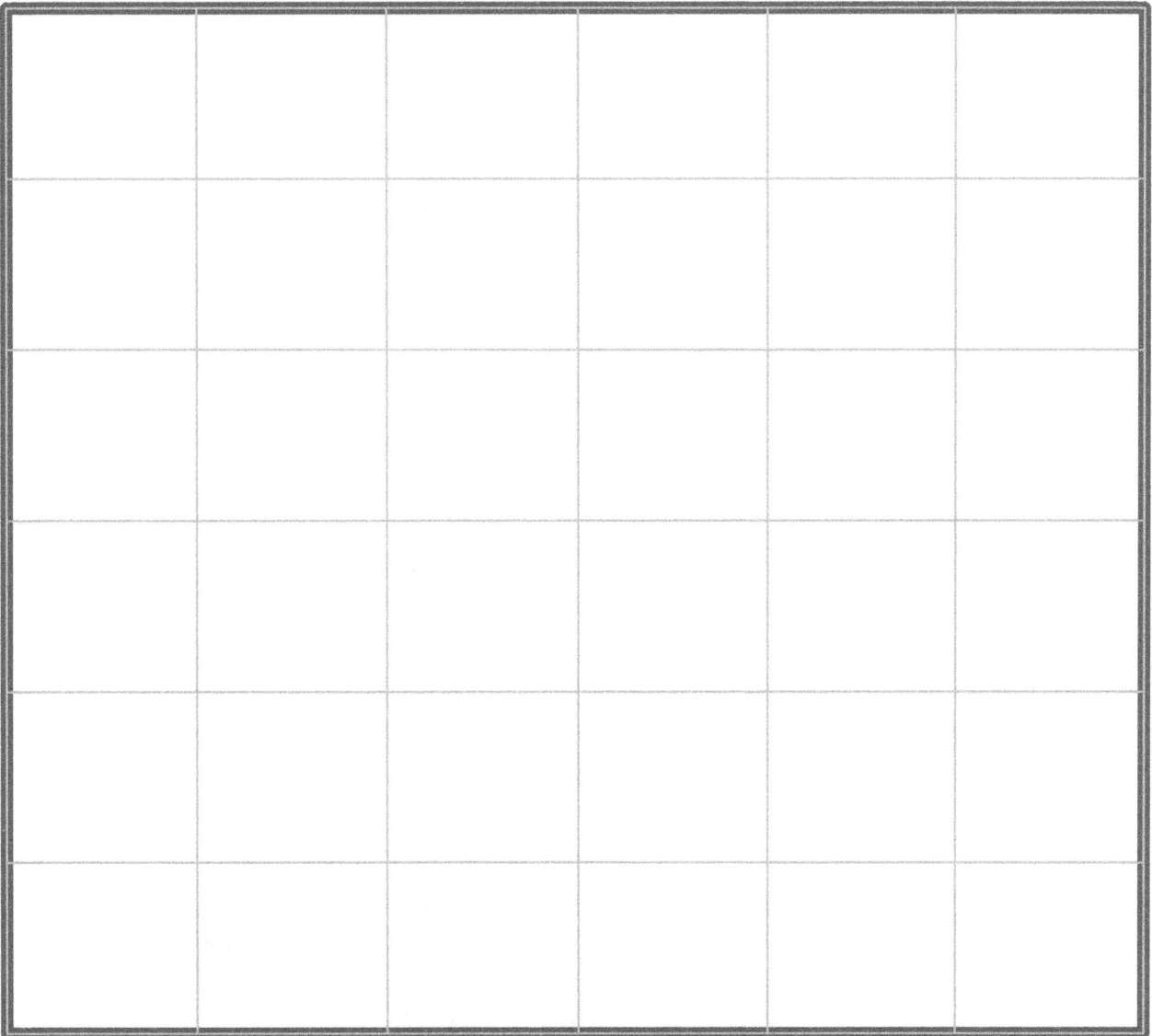

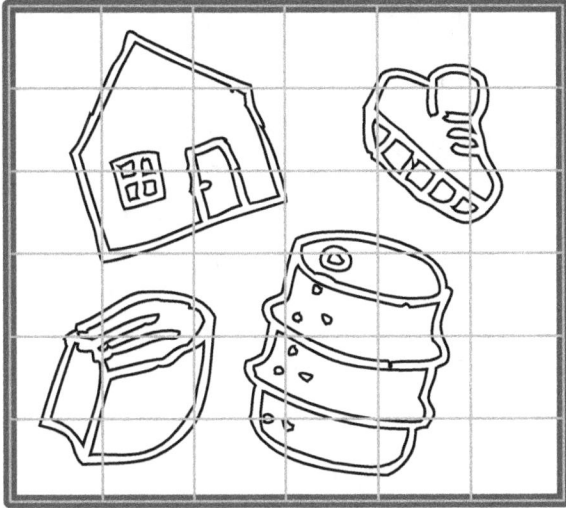

DRAW
THE
IMAGE

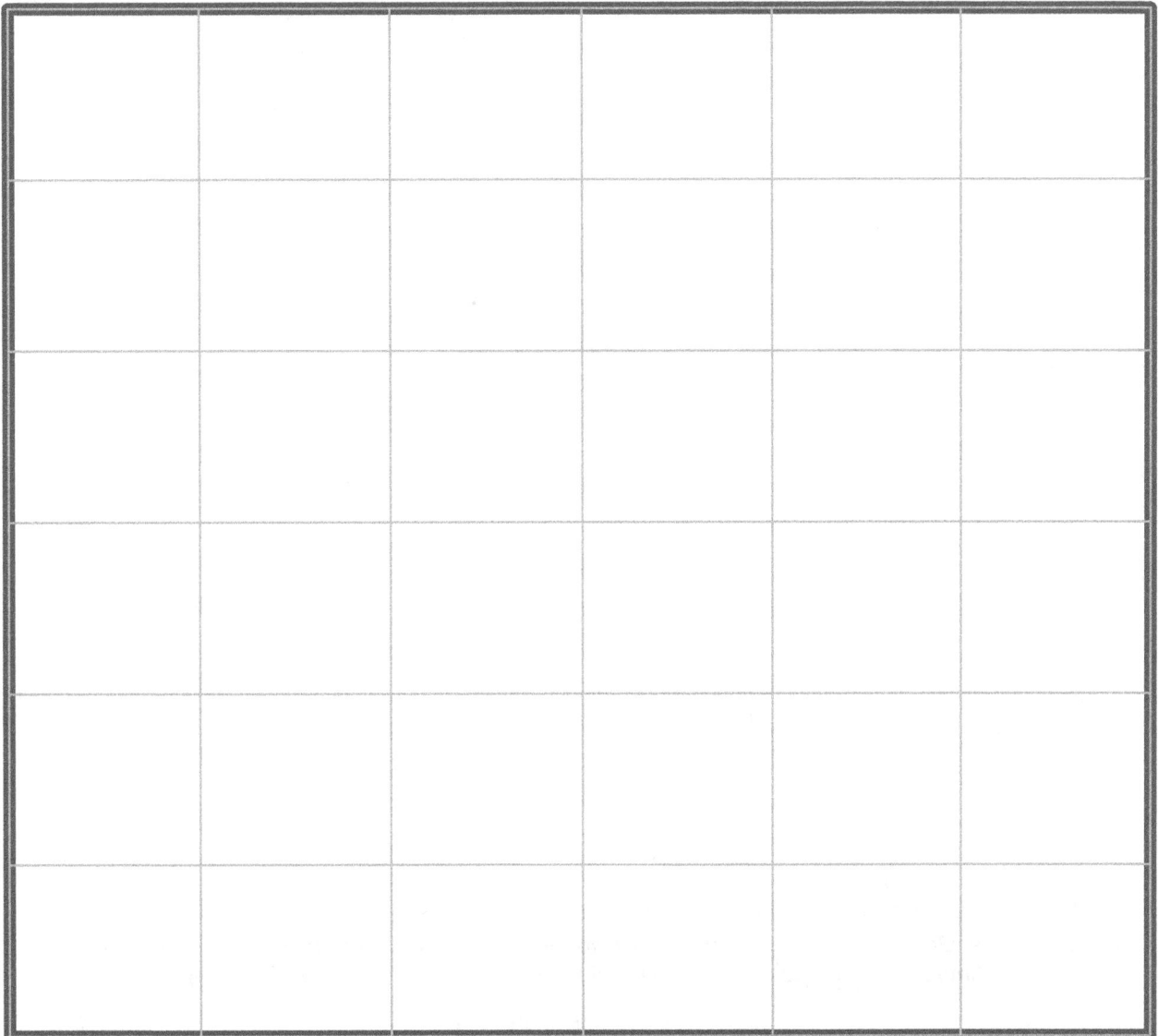

DRAW
THE
IMAGE

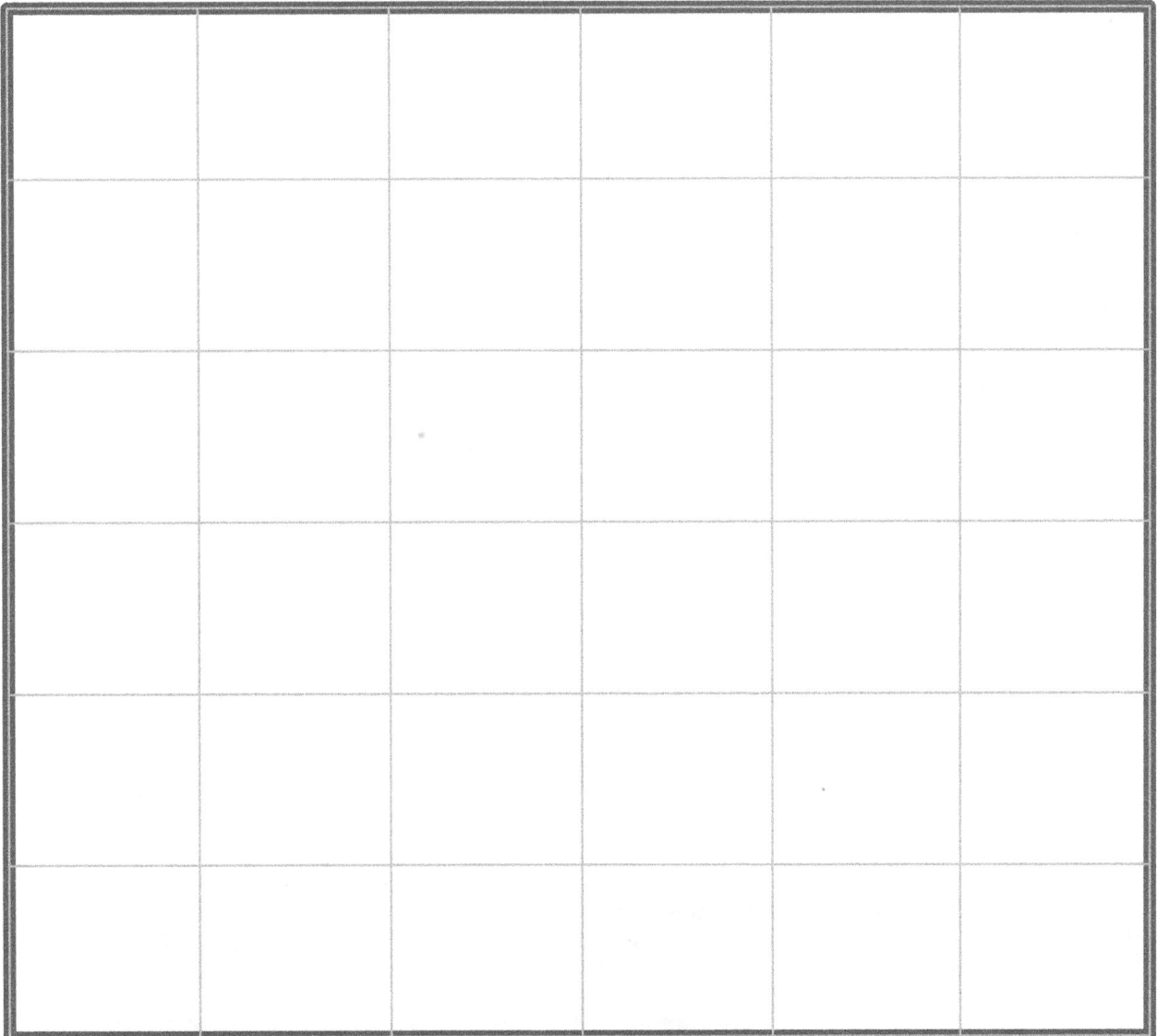

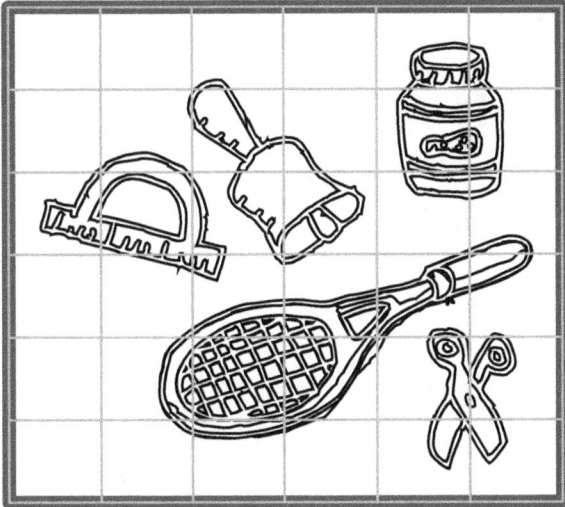

DRAW
THE
IMAGE

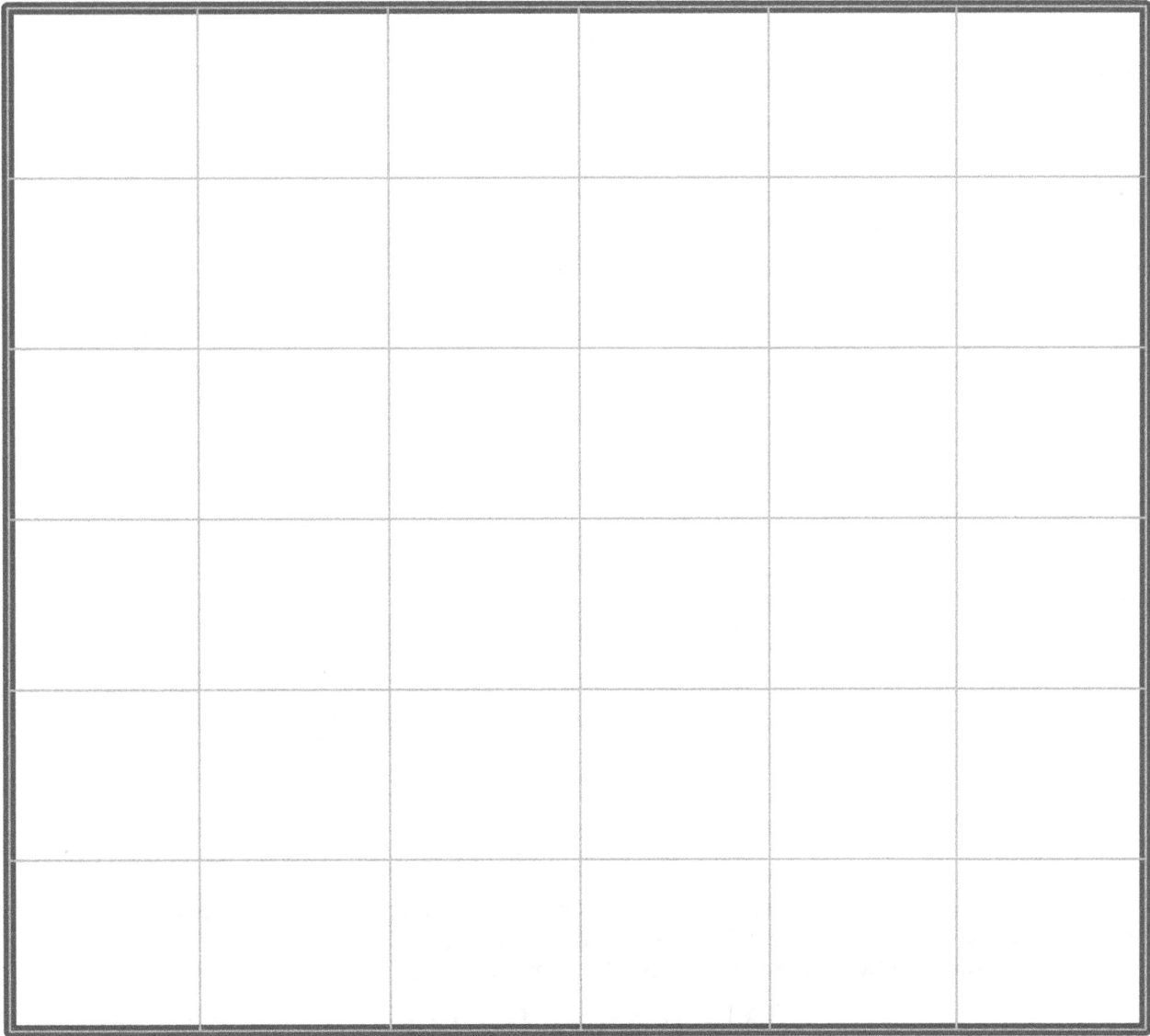

DRAW
THE
IMAGE

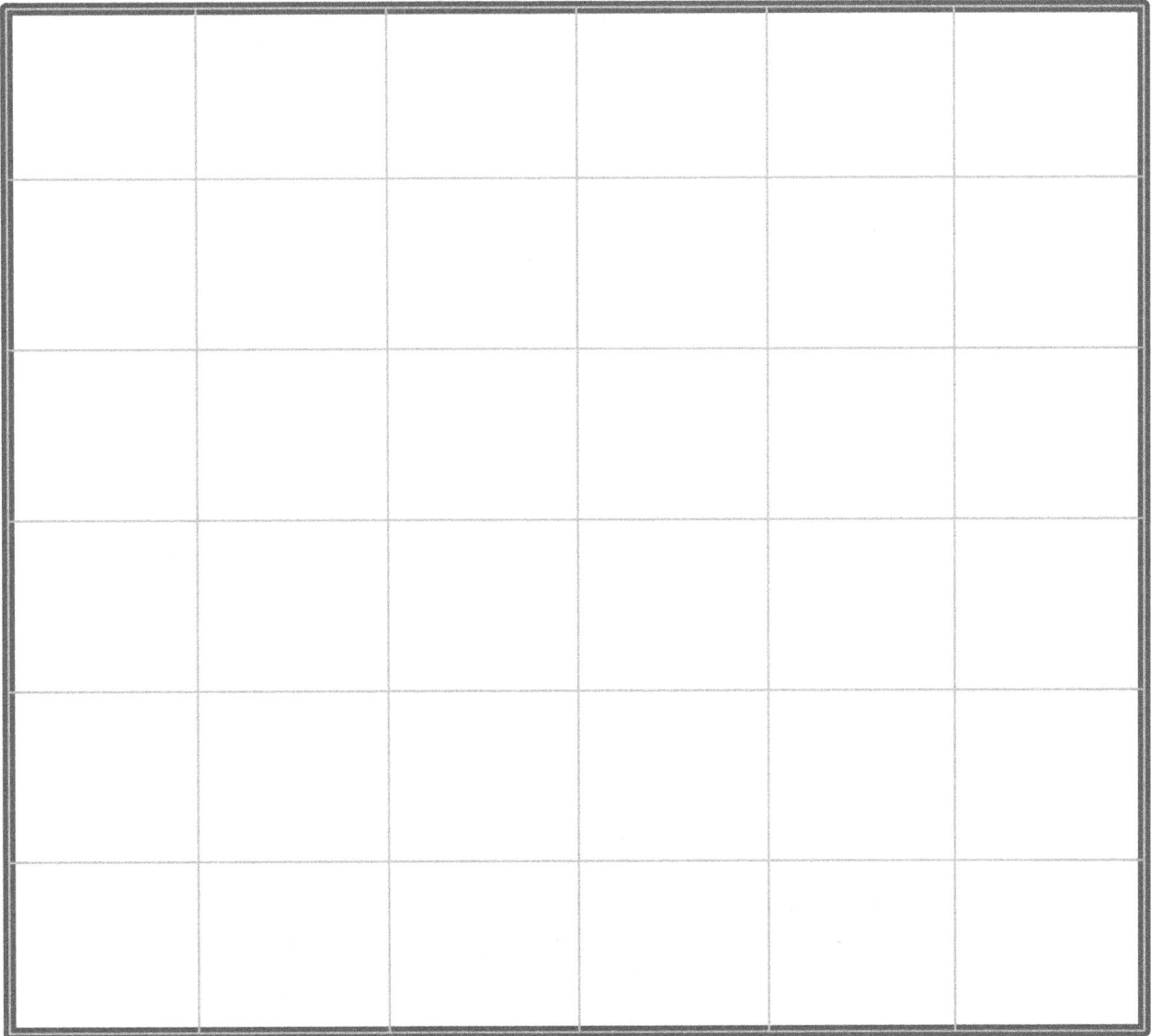

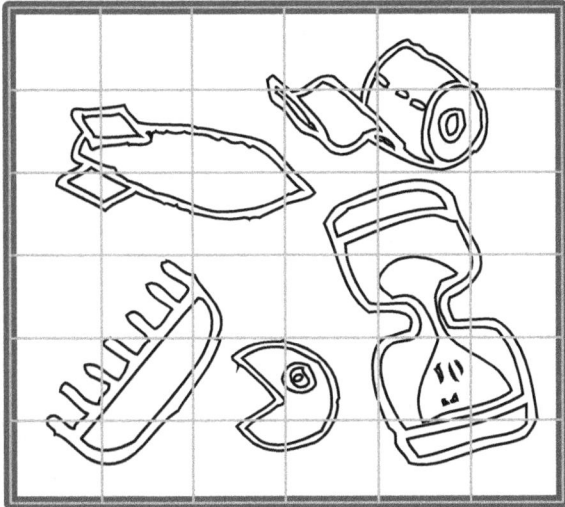

DRAW
THE
IMAGE

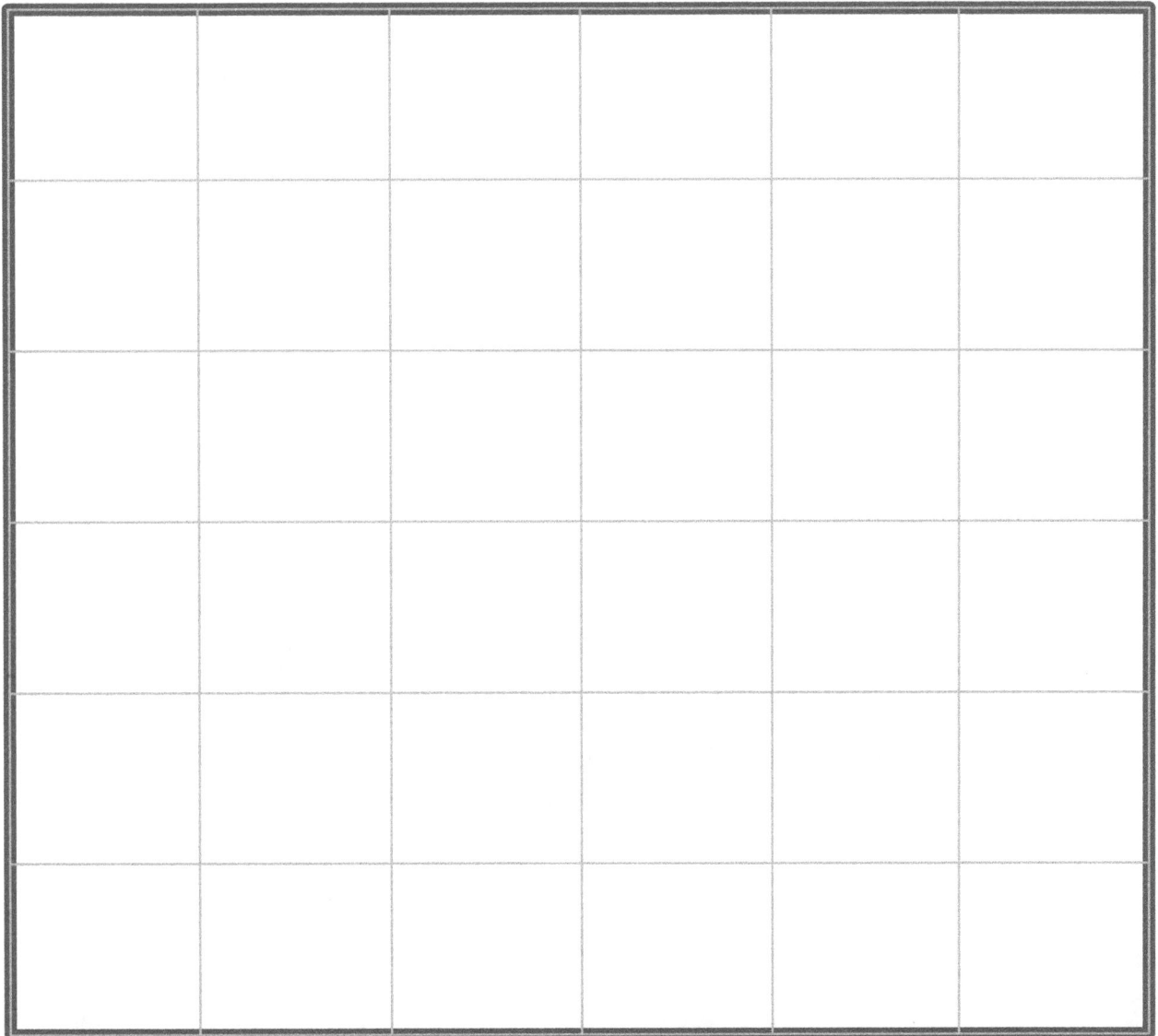

www.ingramcontent.com/pod-product-compliance
Lightning Source LLC
Chambersburg PA
CBHW081338090426
42737CB00017B/3205